WORDS & WORLDS

A STUDY GUIDE FOR COMMUNICATIVE ENGLISH II

M. SARANYA, S. KAVITHA

Made with ♥ on the Notion Press Platform
www.notionpress.com

Contents

Acknowledgements

The journey of writing this book has been an incredibly rewarding experience, and I am deeply grateful to all those who have supported and guided me throughout this process.

First and foremost, I would like to express my heartfelt thanks to my family, whose unconditional love, patience, and belief in me have been my greatest source of strength. Their unwavering support allowed me to dedicate myself to this project with full focus, and for that, I am forever grateful. To my loved ones, who stood by me through the many challenges of this endeavor.

I would like to extend my sincere appreciation to my mentors and teachers, whose wisdom, expertise, and constructive guidance were invaluable throughout this journey. I am privileged to have learned from their vast knowledge and experience.

I am also deeply thankful to my colleagues, friends, and peers, whose collaborative spirit and intellectual input have greatly enriched this book.My profound thanks go to the publishing team for their exceptional professionalism and dedication. deeply appreciate their support throughout the publication process.

I am also grateful to all the scholars, writers, and thinkers whose works and ideas laid the foundation for this book. The depth of their knowledge and the breadth of their thought have inspired me throughout my research and writing.

Finally, to my readers—this book is dedicated to you. Thank you for selecting this one!

M. Saranya

ACKNOWLEDGEMENT

I express my deepest gratitude to everyone who contributed to the creation of this book. Their support, encouragement, and expertise have been invaluable throughout this journey.

First and foremost, I extend heartfelt thanks to my family and friends, whose unwavering belief in my abilities has been a constant source of motivation.

I am profoundly grateful to my mentors and colleagues for their guidance, constructive feedback, and shared wisdom, which have enriched this work. Their insights and suggestions have been instrumental in shaping the content and structure of this book.

Special thanks are due to the publishers and editors for their professional support and dedication, ensuring this book reaches its readers in its best form.

Lastly, I acknowledge the inspiration drawn from the works of countless scholars and writers, whose contributions to this field have paved the way for the ideas presented here.

To my readers, thank you for choosing this book. It is my hope that it serves as a valuable resource and a source of inspiration for your learning and growth.

S. Kavitha

Preface

Language is not merely a tool for communication; it is an art form that connects people, cultures, and ideas. This textbook, *Words and Worlds A study guide for Communicative English II*, is a comprehensive guide to mastering communicative English, blending the beauty of literature with the practicality of language skills. Designed for students and language enthusiasts, this book explores the richness of English through poetry, prose, and drama while building a solid foundation in grammar and writing comprehension.

The structure of the book reflects a systematic approach to learning, beginning with foundational concepts and progressing to advanced topics. Each chapter integrates theoretical knowledge with practical exercises, ensuring learners develop a balanced understanding of grammar, vocabulary, pronunciation, and communication strategies.

This book caters to a wide range of learners, from students aspiring to excel academically to professionals seeking to improve their workplace communication skills. It is also a valuable resource for teachers looking for comprehensive and adaptable materials to support their instructional goals. We hope that this textbook serves as a reliable guide and an inspiring companion in your journey to mastering English. The lessons and skills acquired here aim to not only improve your language proficiency but also empower you to express yourself with clarity and confidence in diverse situations.

Happy Learning!

M. Saranya

Contents

CONTENTS

CHAPTER I

OF ADVERSITY
-FRANCIS BACON

Text

It was a high speech of Seneca (after the manner of the Stoics) that 'the good things that belong to prosperity are to be wished, but the good things that belong to adversity are to be admired'.28 Certainly, if miracles are the command over nature, they appear most in adversity. It is a still higher speech of his than the other (much too high for a heathen) 'It is true greatness to have in one ·person· the frailty of a man and the security of a God' (Vere magnum habere fragilitatem hominis securitatem Dei [ibid. 93]. . . . This is in effect the thing that is depicted in that strange fiction of the ancient poets, Stesichorus, Apollodorus and others, according to which the mighty hero Hercules sailed in a cup. . . . [Bacon goes on about this, saying that this supposed adventure of Hercules 'has some approach to the state of a Christian', in that Hercules' journey resembles 'Christian resolution that sails in the frail bark of the flesh through the waves of the world'. He continues:]. . . .The virtue of prosperity is temperance, the virtue of adversity is fortitude, which in morals is the more heroic virtue. Prosperity is the blessing of the Old Testament, adversity is the blessing of the New, which carries the greater benediction and the clearer revelation of God's favour. Yet even in the Old Testament, if you listen to David's harp, you will hear as many funereal airs as carols; and the pencil of the Holy Ghost has laboured more in describing the afflictions of Job than ·in describing· the felicities of

Solomon. Prosperity is not without many fears and unpleasantnesses; and adversity is not without comforts and hopes. We see in needleworks and embroideries that it is more pleasing to have a lively work on a sad and solemn ground than to have a dark and melancholy work on a lively ground; judge, therefore, of the pleasure of the heart by the pleasure of the eye. Certainly, virtue is like precious odours, most fragrant when they are incensed, or crushed; for prosperity best reveals vice, whereas adversity best reveals virtue.

Glossary

1. **Adversity** – Hardship or difficulty; challenges that test one's resilience.
2. **Prosperity** – A state of wealth, success, or flourishing; often associated with comfort and ease.
3. **Fortitude** – Strength and courage in the face of adversity; the moral virtue of enduring difficulties with resolve.
4. **Temperance** – Moderation and self-restraint, especially in behavior or indulgence.
5. **Benediction** – A blessing, especially one that conveys divine favor or grace.
6. **Hearse-like airs** – Mournful or somber melodies, suggesting sorrow or lamentation.
7. **Revelation** – A divine or profound disclosure; in this context, a clearer understanding of God's will or truth.
8. **Incensed** – Subjected to fire or heat; metaphorically, something that is refined or revealed under pressure.
9. **Virtue** – Moral excellence; qualities such as courage, honesty, and integrity.
10. **Tranquility**: A state of calmness or peacefulness

Francis Bacon (1561–1626) was an English philosopher, statesman, scientist, and essayist. Often regarded as the father of empiricism, Bacon championed the scientific method and inductive reasoning. His works, including *The Essays*, combine practical wisdom with deep insight into human nature and society. Bacon held significant political roles, including Attorney General and Lord Chancellor of England. Despite his contributions, his career ended in disgrace due to allegations of corruption. His writings continue to influence philosophy, science, and literature.

Summary

Bacon opens the essay with the saying of Seneca, a Roman philosopher. He was a great nobleman, from 54 AD to 62 AD, with intense wisdom. He was a writer, philosopher, statesman and a counselor who help people to face suffering and challenges with courage. Bacon quotes his saying in a memorable speech that prosperity is always related to good things, such as happiness and relief, however, the good things that are related to adversity (bad times) should be appreciated as it shapes our personality in a positive manner. Bacon continues his argument with a Latin saying “Bona rerum secundarum optabilia; adversarum mirabilia”, meaning “things of victory are desired, opposing wonderful”. Bacon, by arguing about this point, wants us to think about adversity in a positive way; human should master to deal bliss and misery equally.

It is often seen that most of the miracle happens in the time of adversity. They happen so to completely neutralize the pain of the calamity. Bacon argues about the “faith” of a man. It is in the hands of the God to bring the calamity, and it is in his hand to bring relief from it. We have a faith that everything he does is for the goodness of his creation. He again mentions the Latin proverb meaning that the true greatness is to have the frailty of man to ask for the security of God. It is the true greatness that a powerless, weak man searches for protection in God.

Bacon further says that one can easily find miracles in the poetry. Calamities are the part of life and one cannot get over it as far as he is living. These calamities make it hard for us to have imagination. Through imagination, we can take us away from the harsh realities of life. Moreover, adversities help us to strengthen our imagination by the use of the medium such as poetry to express them.

Bacon, by referring to the Hercules and Prometheus to emphasize the virtue of bravery and fortitude. Prometheus was a monster but was great compassionate toward humans. Bacon uses the metaphor of "ocean" to show the hardship faced by the Prometheus when his torch, with which he lit the fire for humans, was sailed by Hercules. And the Hercules after sailing in the ocean find Prometheus having the torch.

Bacon says that prosperity brings temperance (moderation) while the virtue of adversity is that it brings fortitude (courage in pain) with itself. Both of these come hands to hand and are gifts of God. As prosperity is the sacred sign of old testimony while adversity is the sacred sign of new testimony; however, adversity is superior and is an expression of God benevolent nature. Bacon refers to the Bible and narrates the story of hardship in the life of the Job. A Job was a religious man who faced too much adversity in his life. By referring to this example, Bacon argues that if a man like a Job can face such adversities then why not a common man? Rather we should be thankful to God who makes our life worth living by giving us such adversities. Bacon, in the end, argues that it is not necessary that prosperity will always be accompanied by joy and happiness; similarly, it is not always necessary that adversity will be accompanied by sorrow and grief nor it is not always barren and hopeless. For instance, an embroidery work upon a sad and solemn ground might be attractive but a dark and depressed work on the lightsome ground will never be attractive. Bacon advised that one should go for what his heart feel joyous not for what his eyes find attractive. By taking one side, the side of adversity, bacon says that scent intensifies its odor when it is crushed. By prosperity, one might discover the vice, but adversity helps to discover virtue.

Of Adversity Analysis

GENRE:

"Of Adversity" is Bacon's argumentative essay in which he compares and contrasts between prosperity and adversity and draws the reader's attention towards the positivity that adversity brings with it.

CRITICAL APPRECIATION:

Bacon's essays reflect the style of brevity and wit. His writing is direct and to the point, complete in sense and avoiding too much detail. Bacon has a systematic style, moves rationally from one point to another. The subject matters and ideas of his essays are based on real life. We found Greek and Latin proverbs in his essay of what an educated person might be familiar. In his essays, Bacon always discusses the pons and cons of the subject matter under study and helps the reader to think rationally with his arguments, justifications, and examples from real life and Literature.

All the characteristics discussed above are found in his essay Of Adversity. He represents himself as a true child of Renaissance. Of Adversity, being a penchant essay, not only has a literary value but also has social importance.

In order to make his argument rational, Bacon takes help of religious scriptures, which seems to be very effective. Bacon conveyed his idea in a simple language with the use of simile and metaphors from the common experiences. This essay is the best example of his keen insight into human nature.

His essay is divided into following parts:

· To Admire Adversity:

Prosperity is always related to good things, such as happiness and relief, however, the good things that are related to adversity (bad times) should be appreciated as it shapes our personality in a positive manner.

· True Greatness:

Bacon argues about the "faith" of a man. It is in the hands of the God to bring the calamity, and it is in his hand to bring relief from it. We have a faith that everything he does is for the goodness of his creation. It is the true greatness that a powerless, weak man searches for protection in God.

· Adversity and Poetry:

The calamities in our life make it hard for us to have imagination. Through imagination, we can take us away from the harsh realities of life. So, adversities help us to strengthen our imagination by the use of the medium such as poetry to express them.

· Virtues of Adversity:

Bacon says that prosperity brings temperance (moderation) while the virtue of adversity is that it brings fortitude (courage in pain) with itself. Both of these come hands to hand and are gifts of God. As prosperity is the sacred sign of old testimony while adversity is the sacred sign of new testimony; however, adversity is superior and is an expression of God benevolent nature.

· Adversity Better than Prosperity:

Bacon argues that it is not necessary that prosperity will always be accompanied by joy and happiness; similarly, it is not always necessary that adversity will be accompanied by sorrow and grief nor it is not always barren and hopeless. For instance, an embroidery work upon a sad and solemn ground might be attractive but a dark and depressed work on the lightsome ground will never be attractive. Bacon advised that one should go for what his heart feel joyous not for what his eyes find attractive. By taking one side, the side of adversity, bacon says that scent intensifies its odor when it is crushed. By prosperity, one might discover the vice, but adversity helps to discover the virtue.

Choose the correct answer:

1. What does Bacon consider the virtue of adversity?
   a) Prosperity b) Temperance c) Fortitude d) Vice
2. According to Bacon, what virtue does prosperity reveal?
   a) Courage b) Temperance c) Resilience d) Vice
3. What is adversity compared to in Bacon's essay?
   a) A blessing of the Old Testament
   b) The fragrant smell of crushed odors
   c) The hearse-like airs of David's harp
   d) The fears and distastes of prosperity
4. Which Testament does Bacon associate with adversity?
   a) Old Testament b) New Testament c) Both Testaments
   d) Neither Testament
5. What is the main theme of *Of Adversity*?
   a) The dangers of prosperity
   b) The moral superiority of adversity
   c) The fleeting nature of life
   d) The inevitability of suffering

6. Which biblical figure does Bacon mention as an example of adversity?
   a) Solomon b) Job c) David d) Both b and c
7. How does Bacon describe prosperity?
   a) Free of worries and fears
   b) Full of distastes and insecurities
   c) The ultimate blessing
   d) The clearer revelation of God's favor
   Answer: b) Full of distastes and insecurities
8. What metaphor does Bacon use to illustrate the beauty of adversity?
   a) Needleworks on solemn ground
   b) Hearse-like airs of David's harp
   c) Felicities of Solomon
   d) Odors in prosperity
9. What role does adversity play according to Bacon?
   a) It obscures virtue b) It reveals vice c) It discovers virtue d) It diminishes hope
10. Why does Bacon consider adversity to carry a greater benediction?
    a) It is associated with material wealth
    b) It offers clearer divine revelation
    c) It eliminates moral struggle
    d) It prevents human suffering
11. Which work is considered one of Francis Bacon's most famous essays?
    a) Of studies b) Utopia c) Paradise Lost d) The Prince
12. Which profession did Francis Bacon hold during his lifetime?
    a) Attorney General b) Bishop c) Merchant d) Professor
13. What major historical shift was Bacon's work influential in?
    a) Industrial Revolution b) French Revolution

CHARACTER IS DESTINY – S.RADHAKRISHNAN

The times ahead of us are of a very difficult character. The movements which took place in other countries during a span of centuries have all occurred here more or less simultaneously. What answer to the renaissance, the reformation, the industrial revolution or the political revolution - all those things have been telescoped, so to say, in these few years in our country. If we wish to follow up political revolution by a social and economic one, our universities must send out batches of scientists, technicians, engineers, agriculturists etc. These are essential for changing the face of our country, the economic character of our society. But we not believe that science and technology alone are not enough. There are other countries, much advanced countries in the world, which have achieved marvellous progress in the scientific and technological side, but yet they are torn by strife and they are unable to bring about peace, safety and security of their own people. It only shows that other qualities are also necessary besides those developed by science and technology.

Science is also regarded as a branch of philosophy. The function of the universities is not merely to send out technically skilled and professionally competent men, but it is their duty to produce in them the quality of compassion; the quality which enables the individuals to treat one another in a truly democratic spirit. Our religions have proclaimed from the very beginning that each human individual is to be regarded as a spark of the divine. Twat tam asi, that art thou, is the teaching of the Upanishads. The Buddhists declare that each individual has in him a spark of the divine and could become a bodhisattva. There is a great verse which says that in this poison tree of samsara are two fruits of incomparable value. They are the enjoyment of great books and the company of good souls. If we want to absorb the fruits of great literature, we must read them, read them not as we do cricket stories but read them with concentration. Our generation in its rapid travel has not achieved the habit of reading the great books and has lost the habit of being influenced by the great classics of our country. If these principles of democracy in our constitution are to become habits of mind and patterns of behaviour, principles which change the very character of the individual and the nature of the society, it can be done only by the study of great literature, of philosophy and religion.

That is why even though our country needs great scientists, great technologists, great engineers, we should not neglect to make them humanists. While we retain science and technology we must remember that science and technology are not all. We must note the famous statement that merely by becoming literate without the development of compassion we become demoniac. So no university can regard itself as a true university unless it sends out young men and women who are not only learned but whose hearts are full of compassion for suffering humanity. Unless that is there the university education must be regarded as incomplete. Here is a country which we are interested in building up. For whatever service we take up, we should not care for what we receive. We should know how much we can put into that service. That should be the principle which should animate our young men and women. Ours is a great country. We have had for centuries a great history. The whole of the east reflects our culture. We have to represent what India taught right from the time of Mohenjo-Daro and Harappa. Whether in domestic affairs or in international affairs we must adhere to certain standards. My advice to the young men and women: mother India expects of you that your lives should be clean, noble and dedicated to selfless work.

Notes

About the Author

Dr. S. Radhakrishnan (1888 - 1975) was a scholar, statesman and philosopher. He was born on 5th September and his birthday is observed as teachers' day to honour him. He was the first Indian scholar to teach at the prestigious oxford university where hitherto Indians had gone only as students. He was the vice chancellor of the Andhra University and Benares Hindu University. He became the president of India in 1962. His works include Indian philosophy, an idealist view of life, the Hindu view of life, eastern religions and western thought and recovery of faith. In this essay Dr. Radhakrishnan explores the notion that an individual's character determines their fate, rather than external circumstances or luck. He argues that character is built through consistent thoughts, actions, and moral discipline, forming the foundation of a purposeful and meaningful life.

Summary

The former president Dr. Sarvapalli Radhakrishan in his convocation address stresses the importance of good character. "Character is Destiny" is the essay taken from "The Present Crisis of Faith". Dr. Radhakrishnan says that the nature of the character decides the future. The fate of nation is dependent on the character of the people. The right thinking and right conduct are the foundation of life. He explains the power of a strong character with honesty, courage and discipline. Dr Radhakrishnan helps

Westerners understand "the greatness of Indian culture." He explains that science and technology must be studied along with great literature, philosophy, and religion.

Big changes like the Renaissance, the Reformation, the political revolution, and the industrial revolution are happening all at once in India. To keep up with these huge changes, universities must keep making more and more scientists and technicians.

Science alone cannot solve one's problems. Democracy should not be in paper but in ways of thinking and acting. Radhakrishnan tells students to focus on their studies of literature and philosophy and not read them like cricket stories. Dr. S. Radhakrishan says that a university education isn't complete if it only teaches science and technology and doesn't teach them how to be good people. Men who don't have compassion will turn into demons. A college education that doesn't teach about humanism isn't complete. He also says that a university is like a family, where trade union mentality has no place. Radhakrishnan tells students that developing their character is the most important thing they can do. The future of a country depends on the character of its people. Without good character one cannot achieve greatness. We cannot climb a mountain if the ground at our feet is shaky. In the same way, if your character is bad, you won't get very far.

Radhakrishnan tells students to work hard and not expect anything in return. They should have high standards to live by. They should be clean, kind, and committed to doing work for other people. Also be selfless whilw helping others.

Thus, in this essay "Character is Destiny" Dr. S. Radhakrishnan explains how the character shapes destiny of the nations.

Choose the correct Answer

1. According to Radhakrishnan, what shapes an individual's destiny?

A) Luck B) Wealth C) Character D) Education

2. Which philosophical concept does Radhakrishnan's essay draw upon to explain the relationship between character and destiny?

A) Maya B) Moksha C) Karma D) Nirvana

3. Radhakrishnan emphasizes that character is developed through:

A) Genetics B) Consistent practice and ethical behavior

C) Wealth and power D) Social status

4. What does Radhakrishnan imply is essential for a harmonious society?

A) Economic growth B) Technological advancement

C) Leaders with strong moral character D) Military power

5. What theme is reflected in the statement 'character is destiny'?

A) Fate is entirely predetermined by external forces.

B) Inner moral qualities shape one's future and life path.

C) Success depends solely on intelligence.

D) Material possessions determine one's destiny.

6. How does Radhakrishnan view challenges in life?

A) As obstacles to avoid at all costs

B) As tests that help reveal and strengthen one's character

C) As random occurrences with no purpose

D) As punishments for past actions

7. According to the essay, what is more significant than external circumstances?

A) Wealth B) Fame C) Personal choices and moral integrity D) Education

HOW I TAUGHT MY GRANDMOTHER TO READ
-SUDHA MURTHY

Introduction

How I Taught My Grandmother to Read? is a fictional short story written by prolific Indian author Sudha Murthy. This story was published in the book How I Taught My Grandmother to Read and Other Stories in the year 2004 by Penguin Books, India.

Summary

A girl around the age of twelve is the narrator. She and her grandmother reside in an area in northern Karnataka. In the Kannada language, Triveni is a highly well-known author. She writes beautifully, using clear, approachable language. Her tales explored the complicated issues that surrounded ordinary people. Kashi Yatra, one of her novels, is published as a serial in the Kannada magazine Karmaveera, which is sent out every Wednesday. It was the tale of an elderly woman who yearned to visit Kashi. There was a small orphan girl in the story "Kashi Yatra" as well. She was unable to get married since she lacked the necessary money. The elderly woman ultimately donates all of her savings to the orphan girl which were meant for her to visit Kashi. In the hope that helping an orphan girl is far more important and virtuous than visiting Kashi.

Grandmother never attended school. She was therefore unable to read or write. Hence she would request her 12-year-old granddaughter to read the upcoming Kashi Yatra episode aloud to her. She would pay close attention while She would lose all memory of her work throughout that period. Later, she learned the entire text by heart. The grandmother didn't visit Kashi either. She related to the novel's lead character on a personal level. She later met with her companions in the temple courtyard and discussed the novel with her friends. While the narrator traveled to a nearby village with her cousins for a wedding. She went there for a few days but ended up staying for a week. When she came back, she was shocked to discover her Grandmother crying. Even in the most trying situations, she had never seen her cry. Grandmother continues to explain to her granddaughter, also the narrator of the story, how her mother died when she was very young. Nobody was there to take care of her and educate her. Her father got remarried. Nobody cared about educating girls back then. She therefore never attended school. She had kids after a fairly young marriage. She eventually had grandkids. She enjoyed feeding and cooking for all of her grandchildren, but she occasionally regretted not getting an education for herself. She therefore ensured that her kids and grandchildren went to school but among all of that, she forgot about herself.

Karmaveera arrived as usual while the narrator was gone. She took the magazine out. Everything that was written there was incomprehensible to her. She experienced extreme dependence and helplessness for the first time. She then made the decision to start learning the Kannada alphabet the next day. She chose to put in a lot of effort. She set a deadline for the Saraswati Pooja day during Dassara. She desired independence. The narrator at first laughed at her but seeing her determination started teaching her. The narrator began her tutoring the following day. Grandma excelled in learning. Her homework was outstanding. She would recite, write, read, and repeat.

As usual, the Dassara celebration arrived. By then, Kashi Yatra, a novel, had been released. The novel was purchased by the narrator discreetly. On the day of the pooja, Grandmother forced her granddaughter to sit down on a stool after calling her to the puja site. She handed her material for a frock and then she did something unusual. She knelt down and touched her granddaughter's feet. The narrator was startled by this. Grandmother explains how she was not touching her granddaughter's feet but those of a teacher and her Guru. She was so well taught by her that she could read any novel with confidence. She then opened the book and saw the author's name: Triveni, Kashi Yatra. Grandmother had passed with flying colors.

How I Taught My Grandmother to Read | Analysis

This story demonstrates the humility needed to learn at any age from anyone, as well as the willingness to learn. It shows that learning is a lifelong process and that it cannot be divided into different age groups. It is not necessary for someone to stop studying if they did not receive their education from the ground up throughout the early stages of their lives. With effort, anyone can learn anything, anyplace. Grandmother raised her family her entire life, but she was never given the chance to study. She asked the author to go with her inside the temple on the day of her graduation. The Grandmother knelt down to touch her feet. She did this as a means to honor her teacher, who also happened to be her granddaughter. This represents the value of culture and the idea that respect should be shown to everyone. Despite her surprise, the author accepted the gift because she understood that learning transcended age, gender, and cultural background. The story's main lessons center on the commitment to learning. It requires effort, but it also requires determination, humility, and hard work. She wouldn't have been able to learn if the grandmother had felt that her granddaughter was too young or inexperienced to teach her.

The grandmother serves as a metaphor for learning, aspiration for success, the value of reading and education, and the necessity of education for total dependence in the world we live in. It is evident from this that author Sudha Murty placed a strong emphasis on the value of literacy, education, and dependence throughout the entire story. She wrote in a very direct and realistic style to make her story understandable to a wider variety of people. The use of descriptive language to paint a mental image for the reader, as in the sentence "And she saw the letters dance." When the grandmother could read once again, the narrator compared her to a child to illustrate how pure the grandmother's joy is.

"And the book was like a doorway to a new world." It's like now having learned the grandmother saw the world with an entirely new light. The idea that learning may happen at any age was one of the primary themes. It is demonstrated by the grandmother's character, who chooses to learn at the age of 62. There is a strong message here for all readers. When one is committed to learning, there is no place for disappointment.

The grandmother, who was 62 years old, is depicted in the story touching her granddaughter's feet because she is her mentor and teacher. There shouldn't be any ego or pride involved when one needs to learn and grow.

Glossary

1. Kashi Yatre – A fictional serialized story within the narrative, symbolizing the pursuit of dreams.
2. Karmaveera – A Kannada magazine, central to the plot that serialized *Kashi Yatre*.

3. Protagonist – The young girl narrating the story and teaching her grandmother to read.
4. Illiterate – Unable to read or write; the condition of the grandmother before learning.
5. Determination – Firmness of purpose; the grandmother's resolve to learn despite challenges.
6. Empowerment – The process of becoming stronger and more confident, particularly in controlling one's life.
7. Generational Dynamics – Relationships and interactions between people of different generations, a key element in the story.
8. Autobiographical – Based on the author's own life experiences, as this story partly is.
9. Societal Norms – Rules and expectations within society, which the grandmother challenges by seeking education at her age.
10. Reversal of Roles – The change in traditional roles where the younger teaches and the elder learns.

Choose the correct answer

1. What inspired the grandmother to learn to read?
   a) Her granddaughter's insistence
   b) A serialized story in *Karmaveera*
   c) A neighbor's challenge
   d) Her husband's encouragement
2. What was the title of the serialized story in *Karmaveera*?
   a) *Ramayana* b) *Kashi Yatre* c) *Bhagavad Gita* d) *Mahabharata*
3. How did the grandmother express her gratitude to the protagonist?
   a) She made her favorite dish
   b) She touched her feet

c) She gifted her a sari
d) She wrote her a letter

4. What was the grandmother's main motivation to learn to read?
   a) To challenge societal norms
   b) To gain respect in her village
   c) To read *Kashi Yatre* independently
   d) To set an example for her family
5. What does *Kashi Yatre* symbolize in the story?
   a) The journey of self-discovery
   b) The importance of religion
   c) The grandmother's dreams and aspirations
   d) The bond between the protagonist and her grandmother
6. What gift did the grandmother give her granddaughter after learning to read?
   a) A frock b) A book c) A pencil box d) A proper gurudakshina
7. What societal norm does the grandmother break?
   a) Elders are always teachers
   b) Education is for the young
   c) Women should not be literate
   d) Reading is a waste of time
8. How does the story address the issue of literacy?
   a) It criticizes the lack of literacy programs
   b) It shows how literacy empowers individuals
   c) It focuses on professional education
   d) It highlights literacy as unnecessary for elders.
9. Why does the grandmother's act of touching her granddaughter's feet stand out?
   a) It is against Indian traditions
   b) It shows respect for knowledge regardless of age
   c) It embarrasses the granddaughter

d) It symbolizes her failure

10. How did the grandmother feel after learning to read?
    a) She felt embarrassed to have taken so long
    b) She felt independent and empowered
    c) She regretted the effort it took
    d) She wanted to stop learning

CHAPTER II

THERE'S BEEN A DEATH, IN THE OPPOSITE HOUSE

• EMILY DICKINSON

There's been a Death, in the Opposite House,
As lately as Today —
I know it, by the numb look
Such Houses have — alway —

The Neighbors rustle in and out —
The Doctor — drives away —
A Window opens like a Pod —
Abrupt — mechanically —

Somebody flings a Mattress out —
The Children hurry by —
They wonder if it died — on that —
I used to — when a Boy —

The Minister — goes stiffly in —
As if the House were His —
And He owned all the Mourners — now —
And little Boys — besides —

And then the Milliner — and the Man
Of the Appalling Trade —
To take the measure of the House —

There'll be that Dark Parade —

Of Tassels — and of Coaches — soon —
It's easy as a Sign —
The Intuition of the News —
In just a Country Town —

Summary and Analysis

The poet of "There's been a death, in the opposite house", Emily Dickinson is a notable figure in American poetry and is referred to as a prolific writer who was born on December 10, 1830, in Amherst, U.S, and died in the year 1886. She always had a strong connection with her community. This poem first appeared for printing after her death like most of her other works in A Collection of Posthumous in 1896. Emily Dickinson in this poem successfully explores the theme of death and community. She incorporates a male speaker in the poem and predicts the actions that are being taken in a small town after a person's death.

Death, in this poem, is both ordinary and eerie—and perhaps it's all the more eerie because it's so ordinary. As the poem's speaker watches the people in the house across the road deal with the aftermath of a death, he's able to predict all the rituals that are about to take place, from the doctor's departure to the final "Dark Parade" of the funeral procession. The clockwork predictability of the events around this death only underline the idea that death comes to everyone, sooner or later: these rituals are only familiar because death is unavoidable. Death, this poem's well-worn routines suggest, is an inevitable part of life—and no matter how well one knows this, the thought isn't altogether comfortable.

The speaker of this poem doesn't have to be told that "there's been a Death, in the Opposite House": he can tell just by observing the usual postmortem routine going on over there. As the "Doctor" leaves to be replaced by the "Minister," the speaker can predict all the next steps, right up to the formal "Tassels" and "Coaches" of the funeral procession. Especially in this speaker's small 19th-century "Country Town," death is an ordinary thing, framed by all sorts of predictable and even humdrum rituals. Everything happening across the road is so familiar to the speaker that he doesn't even sound particularly moved or upset by what he sees.

But perhaps the speaker's blasé tone, and even the orderly funeral rituals themselves, are just ways to keep the uncomfortable (and unavoidable) realities of death at bay. As the people in the house throw out an old mattress, the speaker observes children hurrying past and speculates that they "wonder if it died — on that," just as he used to wonder as a child. The use of the word "it" to describe the corpse (rather than "he" or "she") suggests just how uncanny and alien a dead body feels—and the speaker clearly shares the children's unease. Similarly, when the speaker euphemistically describes a mortician as a "Man / Of the Appalling Trade," his indirect language makes it sound as if a mortician's job is too horrific to describe plainly. The conventional bustle of funerals can't quite make death itself seem ordinary.

Death might happen every day, the poem thus suggests, but that doesn't mean it's pleasant to contemplate—especially because there's no avoiding death oneself! Even this speaker, who describes the proceedings in such a detached voice, nevertheless pays close attention all day to what's happening across the road, and sometimes feels "appall[ed]"; he's at a literal and figurative distance from death for now, but that won't last forever. The well-worn, conventional rituals that people use to manage their feelings about death, the poem suggests, might only underline death's uncomfortable inevitability.

Glossary

1. Casket: A small container or box used to hold a dead person's body.
2. Funeral: A ceremony for burying or cremating a dead person.
3. Mourners: People who express sorrow or grief at a death.
4. Shroud: A cloth used to cover a dead body, typically before burial.
5. Toll: The ringing of a bell, typically to mark a death or funeral.
6. Solitude: The state of being alone, often in a peaceful or quiet manner.
7. Grief: A deep sorrow, especially caused by the loss of someone or something important.
8. Eternity: Infinite or unending time, often used in a spiritual or religious context to refer to the afterlife.
9. Tassel: Aecorative bunch of threads, cords, or fibers that are tied together at one end and hang loosely at the other.

Choose the correct answer

1. What is the main event described in the poem?

a) A wedding b) A birth c) A death d) A celebration

2. How does the speaker learn about the death in the opposite house?

a) By hearing the tolling of a bell b) By seeing mourners in the street

c) By a direct message from the family d) By reading an obituary

3. What does the speaker observe about the casket in the poem?

a) It is decorated with flowers b) It is carried by a procession

c) It is taken out of the house and onto a cart d) It is left untouched inside the house

4. How does the speaker react to the event of death in the opposite house?

a) She expresses deep grief

b) She feels indifferent and detached

c) She feels a sense of curiosity and observation

d) She immediately visits the mourning family

5. What is the primary tone of the poem?

a) Joyful and celebratory b) Calm and reflective c) Somber and mournful

d) Excited and anxious

6. What detail in the poem suggests that the death is a serious and sorrowful event?

a) The presence of the family dog

b) The ringing of the death bell and procession

c) The decorations in the opposite house

d) The arrival of the newspaper

7. What does the "shroud" in the poem symbolize?

a) A sense of hope

b) The finality of death

c) The care of the deceased

d) A decoration for the house

8. What role does the "mourners" in the poem play?

a) They are guests at a wedding

b) They are part of the funeral procession

c) They celebrate the life of the deceased

THE SOUL'S PRAYER
-SAROJINI NAIDU

In childhood's pride I said to Thee:
'O Thou, who mad'st me of Thy breath,
Speak, Master, and reveal to me
Thine inmost laws of life and death.
'Give me to drink each joy and pain
Which Thine eternal hand can mete,
For my insatiate soul would drain
Earth's utmost bitter, utmost sweet.
'Spare me no bliss, no pang of strife,
Withhold no gift or grief I crave,
The intricate lore of love and life
And mystic knowledge of the grave.'
Lord, Thou didst answer stern and low:
'Child, I will hearken to thy prayer,
And thy unconquered soul shall know
All passionate rapture and despair.
'Thou shalt drink deep of joy and fame,
And love shall burn thee like a fire,
And pain shall cleanse thee like a flame,
To purge the dross from thy desire.
'So shall thy chastened spirit yearn
To seek from its blind prayer release,
And spent and pardoned, sue to learn
The simple secret of My peace.
'I, bending from my sevenfold height,
Will teach thee of My quickening grace,
Life is a prism of My light,
And Death the shadow of My face.'

Summary

The poet refers to herself as the innocent child of God in the first stanza and expresses pride in being born from His breath. The two greatest mysteries of life and death become her two greatest obsessions at that point. She believes that if God revealed to her the rules and the mysteries of life and death, she could prepare herself for the difficult emotions that come with living, such as joys and sorrows.

In the 2nd stanza, She requests God to provide her with both joy and suffering because she wants to fully experience both. She desires to feel both feelings in her lifetime. The poetess asks God to grant her the ability to feel everything intensely, including all of life's joys and pains. Although she yearns for happiness, she is also willing to endure all of life's hardships.

In the 3rd stanza, she begs God not to withhold any of the joys or sorrows. She yearns for the joy of love and living, which improve our lives, but she also longs to learn the dark secrets of the afterlife. She is happy about it because she is aware that the soul might not have to return to address the wanderer's problems. The knowledge of the grave is mystical since what occurs there is not visible to the naked eye.

In the 4th stanza, God hears the child's prayers and responds in a hushed, solemn voice. He assures the poet that he would consider her demands and that he will endow her soul with knowledge of rapture and despair at their heights. In spite of all these complex feelings, the poet will maintain discipline.

In the 5th stanza, God says that the poetess will experience profound and intense moments of happiness and recognition in her life. Love will have a passionate and consuming effect on her. "And pain shall cleanse thee like a flame" suggests that pain and suffering have a purifying effect on her. Just as a flame purges impurities, the pain endured will cleanse and purify her desires, freeing her from any negative or superficial aspects. "To purge the dross from thy desire" means that pain acts as a catalyst to remove any impurities or superficialities from one's desires. It suggests that going through difficult experiences can refine one's desires, separating what is truly important from what is superficial or insincere. By enduring pain, a person can gain clarity and a deeper understanding of their true desires and aspirations.

In the 6th stanza, God informs her that after experiencing all the joys and sorrows, love and comfort, highs and lows of life, her soul will not be satisfied and will want to be freed from the bonds of blind prayer. Her spirit will then beg to learn about peace rather than passion. It will want to know how to feel calm and quietness without the fire and flame, the burning and purging. The soul will wish to achieve salvation or eternal peace.

In the last stanza, God says that He will guide her by descending from the heavens and unveiling for her the significance of His grace—that even in places where the sun has never shone, there is light—His light. The poet finally finds comfort in the realization that life and death are only the two manifestations of God—His light and shadow. Thus, the poem ends with the belief that life and death are mutually dependent and interlinked with one another.

Analysis

Sarojini Naidu understands that both "good and bad things" in life are necessary for a satisfactory completion of one soul's agenda. First the question Everything is perfect exactly as it is. We can't see the other side because we are not there – but we know that within the frame of time we will get there and be able to see the whole of the mosaic image. At the moment certain things don't make sense; but that doesn't deter Naidu to accept life as it is: with the bitter and the sweet.

This shows great understanding of how the soul uses the body and the body-brain as mere tools to develop spiritually. The spiritually blind will want to reject the painful parts of life, failing to envisage that the only way the soul can be cleansed of residue or simple unorganised illusory perceptions is to have the calling of pain.

Pains serve two important purposes: when knocking at the door they grant vision to our spiritual eyes; as the physical ones can only see the wound and the wound doesn't always present itself when a crack in the thought system needs to be sealed (cleansed). The second purpose of the "pain calling" is to remind us, each and every time, that our little plans and designs won't heal the root of the problem. In a chaotic world God is needed at the root; the soil surpassing any logic within our human limited comprehension of the workings of Truth and Knowledge.

We have been made of God's breath, so our very essence goes further than resembling His. We are his breath and like it, when it is expired (exhalation) we experience human life as it presents itself now; when inspired (inhalation) we make an attempt to go back home through the death of the body. Each breath represents a state in our being, death the beginning of our spiritual life, birth the end of it. Human birth and death imply a simple reversal: spiritual death and birth.

Sajorini writes this poem with the voice of a child and it is impressive to see someone so eager to go back to God (to wake up). By asking God to withhold nothing ("Withhold no gift or grief I crave") she is delighted because the soul might not have to come back to deal with vagabond issues. The knowledge of the grave is mystic ("And mystic knowledge of the grave") because we simply don't know.

What happens at the grave goes beyond our ordinary senses; we can't experience it while in this body. Neither do we remember how it was or what it was before human birth, something needed if we are to work on our toxic character defects with a full blown amount of fairness.

Purity doesn't come at a low price; we must endure the difficulties we chose for this life as souls and live with the consequences of our choices and actions – choices and actions that define us as we go along. Then God answers. God grants Sarojini her wish, and this is interesting because it is what differentiates the boys from the men. The boys cry because God "brings" suffering to the world. The men understand that suffering is only part of the game.

Life is just another "genre" of the Spinning or Cosmic Wheel. This particular version of "us" is played out with drama as well as through time intervals, obvious script techniques needed for our development as central characters. For the "arch" to take place, ups and downs are necessary. A good shaping of this arch determined by our behaviour will make the play more or less dynamic but that doesn't take away the overal theme: spiritual growth expanding into an inevitable awakening. First we need to go through the experience of desiring joy, fame, love. The problems are not in these very things (joy, fame, love), but in the desire we feel for them. Desire pushes us into manipulation, which comes at the price of expectation, which ends in resentment when outcomes are not met. The line fails to be linear and the ups and downs manifesting from our erroneous perception carry pain along the way. Desire, then, is not desirable. It always implies suffering as well as other dirty little tricks like judgement and punishment.

We might have to go through the pain many, many lives. But eventually the lesson is learned – pain "cleanses us like a flame, purging the dross from our desire". The Spirit's yearn, a seeking cry, comes not from us but from God Himself! God cries for us, His children, begging us to come home. The release is a call to the waking up that takes place when blind prayer turns into a sighted realisation: we never actually needed to learn through pain, and there was never anything to fear. Mystic mystery is a simple secret, nothing more. It's God's peace. The last verse discloses a loving God; a God that bends with care to teach His children that where the sun has never shone there is also light, His light. Shadow and Light are just like birth and death, like night and day, like inhaling and exhaling. Pain and joy are just part of the windmills of your mind. And the Mind – deep and calm in its Real state – when filtered through the body is just a memory of something else.

Glossary

1. Soul: The spiritual or immaterial part of a person, often considered the essence of one's being.
2. Prayer: A solemn request for help or expression of thanks addressed to a deity or spirit.
3. Mercy: Compassion or forgiveness shown toward someone whom it is within one's power to punish or harm.
4. Faith: Complete trust or confidence in someone or something.
5. Grief: Sorrow or deep sadness, often due to loss or misfortune.
6. Alone: Having no one else present; solitary.

7. Suffering: The state of undergoing pain, distress, or hardship.
8. Redeem: To save or recover something from a state of ruin or loss.
9. Tears: Drops of clear salty liquid secreted by glands in the eyes, often as a result of emotion.
10. Radiance: Bright light or glow that shines out.
11. Prism: Three-dimensional geometric shape with two parallel
12. Rapture: A feeling of intense joy, delight, or ecstasy
13. yearn: To deeply desire something
14. Purge: Clean

Choose the best Answer

1. What is the central theme of the poem The Soul's Prayer?

a) Nature's beauty
b) The soul's plea for mercy and peace
c) The glory of love
d) The struggles of human existence

2. In the poem, what does the soul ask for from the divine?

a) Wisdom b) Mercy and forgiveness c) Strength d) Wealth

3. What is the tone of the poem The Soul's Prayer?

a) Joyful b) Hopeful c) Somber and pleading d) Angry

4. What does the soul seek through prayer in the poem?

a) A chance to live forever
b) Healing and the end of sorrow
c) Worldly possessions
d) Control over nature

LONDON
- WILLIAM BLAKE

I wander through each chartered street,
Near where the chartered Thames does flow,
And mark in every face I meet
Marks of weakness, marks of woe.

In every cry of every man,
In every infant's cry of fear,
In every voice, in every ban,
The mind-forged manacles I hear.

How the chimney-sweeper's cry
Every black'ning church appalls,
And the hapless soldier's sigh
Runs in blood down palace walls.

But most, through midnight streets I hear
How the youthful harlot's curse
Blasts the new-born infant's tear,
And blights with plagues the marriage hearse.

Glossary

1. Chartered: Controlled, regulated, or mapped (implying restricted freedom).
2. Marks of woe: Visible signs of sorrow and despair.
3. Mind-forged manacles: Metaphor for mental or ideological constraints.
4. Chimney-sweeper: Refers to children forced into dangerous labor cleaning chimneys.
5. Black'ning church: A symbol of the church's moral corruption and complicity in social injustices.
6. Palace walls: Symbolic of the monarchy and ruling elite.

7. Midnight streets: Suggests secrecy, darkness, and despair.
8. Harlot: A young prostitute, representing societal exploitation and moral decay.
9. Curse: The harlot's vulgar language or symbolic representation of disease and suffering.
10. Marriage hearse: An oxymoron implying the death of love and the sanctity of marriage.

About the author

William Blake (1757–1827) was an English poet, painter, and printmaker, regarded as one of the most influential figures of the Romantic Age. Known for his visionary and mystical works, Blake combined poetry and visual art to express his profound philosophical and spiritual ideas. His collections *Songs of Innocence* and *Songs of Experience* explore themes of innocence, corruption, and the dualities of human existence. Though largely unrecognized during his lifetime, Blake's work challenged societal norms, critiqued industrialization, and exposed the injustices of his era. Today, he is celebrated for his innovative artistry and his ability to merge imagination with social commentary. In *London*, William Blake presents a stark portrayal of the suffering and oppression experienced by the people living in the city during the Industrial Revolution. The poem opens with the speaker walking through the "chartered streets" of London, observing the signs of misery in every face he meets. He hears cries of pain from men, children, and infants, reflecting widespread despair. Blake uses the metaphor of "mind-forged manacles" to suggest that people's suffering is not just physical but psychological, stemming from the social systems that bind them. The poem condemns the hypocrisy of institutions like the Church and the monarchy, both of which are complicit in the suffering, symbolized by the "black'ning church" and the blood on "palace walls." Blake ends the poem with an image of a "harlot's curse," which damns both the innocent newborns and the institution of marriage, highlighting how societal ills destroy innocence and corrupt love.

Analysis of "London"

Blake's *London* is a powerful critique of the moral and social decay in the city. The poem is structured around the speaker's walk through London, where he observes the impact of industrialization, inequality, and political corruption on the lives of its citizens. The repetition of the word "chartered" in the first stanza conveys the idea of control and ownership, emphasizing how even nature, represented by the Thames, is commodified. The "marks of weakness" and "marks of woe" on the people's faces symbolize the physical and emotional toll of a society that has lost its humanity. The phrase "mind-forged manacles" is a key element of the poem, as it represents the mental and ideological chains that prevent people from seeing their own oppression and challenging the systems that enforce it. Blake critiques the Church for its failure to alleviate suffering, instead of becoming complicit in it ("black'ning church"). Similarly, the monarchy and the ruling class are depicted as being indifferent to the suffering of the poor, with the "palace walls" stained with the blood of soldiers. In the final stanza, Blake condemns the exploitation of women through prostitution, linking it to the breakdown of familial structures and the loss of innocence, encapsulated in the paradox of the "marriage hearse." This powerful imagery critiques the social and moral corruption of Blake's time, while calling attention to the need for change.

Choose the correct answer

1. What does "chartered Thames" symbolize?
   a) Natural beauty b) Freedom and flow c) Restriction and control
   d) The industrial revolution
2. What do "marks of weakness, marks of woe" refer to?
   a) Physical scars b) Signs of poverty and suffering
   c) Freedom and joy d) Rebellion and anger
3. What is the meaning of "mind-forged manacles"?
   a) Literal chains
   b) Psychological and ideological constraints
   c) Tools of the blacksmith
   d) Weapons of war
4. Who does the "chimney-sweeper" symbolize?
   a) Factory workers b) Child laborers c) Soldiers d) Clergy members
5. What does "black'ning church" imply?
   a) The church's physical appearance
   b) The church's involvement in pollution
   c) The church's moral corruption
   d) A literal black church
6. What does "palace walls" represent?
   a) Freedom and justice
   b) The monarchy and ruling elite
   c) Religious institutions
   d) Urban architecture
7. What is the significance of "midnight streets"?
   a) Celebration and festivities
   b) Darkness and despair
   c) Quietness and peace

d) Economic prosperity

8. Who is the "harlot" in the poem?
   a) A symbol of freedom
   b) A young prostitute representing exploitation
   c) A wealthy woman
   d) A religious figure
9. What does the phrase "marriage hearse" symbolize?
   a) Joyful weddings
   b) Death and decay in relationships
   c) Religious traditions
   d) Prosperity in marriage
10. What is the overall tone of the poem?
    a) Uplifting and hopeful
    b) Critical and somber
    c) Humorous and light-hearted
    d) Optimistic and motivational

CHAPTER III

THE PURLOINED LETTER
-EDGAR ALLEN POE

The Purloined Letter

By Edgar Allan Poe

Nil sapientiae odiosius acumine nimio.
Seneca.

At Paris, just after dark one gusty evening in the autumn of 18—, I was enjoying the twofold luxury of meditation and a meerschaum, in company with my friend C. Auguste Dupin, in his little back library, or book-closet, au troisième, No. 33, Rue Dunôt, Faubourg St. Germain. For one hour at least we had maintained a profound silence; while each, to any casual observer, might have seemed intently and exclusively occupied with the curling eddies of smoke that oppressed the atmosphere of the chamber. For myself, however, I was mentally discussing certain topics which had formed matter for conversation between us at an earlier period of the evening; I mean the affair of the Rue Morgue, and the mystery attending the murder of Marie Rogêt. I looked upon it, therefore, as something of a coincidence, when the door of our apartment was thrown open and admitted our old acquaintance, Monsieur G—, the Prefect of the Parisian police. We gave him a hearty welcome; for there was nearly half as much of the entertaining as of the contemptible about the man, and we had not seen him for several years. We had been sitting in the dark, and Dupin now arose for the purpose of lighting a lamp, but sat down again, without doing so, upon G.'s saying that he had called to consult us, or rather to ask the opinion of my friend, about some official business which had occasioned a great deal of trouble. "If it is any point requiring reflection," observed Dupin, as he forebore to enkindle the wick, "we shall examine it to better purpose in the dark."

"That is another of your odd notions," said the Prefect, who had a fashion of calling every thing "odd" that was beyond his comprehension, and thus lived amid an absolute legion of "oddities." "Very true," said Dupin, as he supplied his visiter with a pipe, and rolled towards him a comfortable chair.

"And what is the difficulty now?" I asked. "Nothing more in the assassination way, I hope?"

"Oh no; nothing of that nature. The fact is, the business is very simple indeed, and I make no doubt that we can manage it sufficiently well ourselves; but then I thought Dupin would like to hear the details of it, because it is so excessively odd." "Simple and odd," said Dupin. "Why, yes; and not exact-

— 1 —

Created for Lit2Go on the web at fcit.usf.edu

ly that, either. The fact is, we have all been a good deal puzzled because the affair is so simple, and yet baffles us altogether."

"Perhaps it is the very simplicity of the thing which puts you at fault," said my friend.

"What nonsense you do talk!" replied the Prefect, laughing heartily. "Perhaps the mystery is a little too plain," said Dupin. "Oh, good heavens! who ever heard of such an idea?" "A little too self-evident." "Ha! ha! ha—ha! ha! ha!—ho! ho! ho!" roared our visiter, profoundly amused, "oh, Dupin, you will be the death of me yet!" "And what, after all, is the matter on hand?" I asked. "Why, I will tell you," replied the Prefect, as he gave a long, steady and contemplative puff, and settled himself in his chair. "I will tell you in a few words; but, before I begin, let me caution you that this is an affair demanding the greatest secrecy, and that I should most probably lose the position I now hold, were it known that I confided it to any one."

"Proceed," said I.

"Or not," said Dupin.

"Well, then; I have received personal information, from a very high quarter, that a certain document of the last importance, has been purloined from the royal apartments. The individual who purloined it is known; this beyond a doubt; he was seen to take it. It is known, also, that it still remains in his possession." "How is this known?" asked Dupin. "It is clearly inferred," replied the Prefect, "from the nature of the document, and from the non-appearance of certain results which would at once arise from its passing out of the robber's possession; that is to say, from his employing it as he must design in the end to employ it."

"Be a little more explicit," I said. "Well, I may venture so far as to say that the paper gives its holder a certain power in a certain quarter where such power is immensely valuable." The Prefect was fond of the cant of diplomacy. "Still I do not quite understand," said Dupin. "No? Well; the disclosure of the document to a third person, who shall be nameless, would bring in question the honor of a personage of most exalted station; and this fact gives the holder of the document an ascendancy over the illustrious personage whose honor and peace are so jeopardized."

"But this ascendancy," I interposed, "would depend upon the robber's knowledge of the loser's knowledge of the robber. Who would dare—" "The thief," said G., "is the Minister D—, who dares all things, those unbecoming as well as those becoming a man. The method of the theft was not less ingenious than bold. The document in question—a letter, to be frank—had been received by the personage robbed while alone in the royal boudoir. During its perusal she was suddenly interrupted by the entrance of the other exalted personage from whom especially it was her wish to conceal it. After a hurried and vain endeavor to thrust it in a drawer, she was forced to place it, open as it was, upon a table. The address, however, was uppermost,

The Purloined Letter

and, the contents thus unexposed, the letter escaped notice. At this juncture enters the Minister D—. His lynx eye immediately perceives the paper, recognises the handwriting of the address, observes the confusion of the personage addressed, and fathoms her secret. After some business transactions, hurried through in his ordinary manner, he produces a letter somewhat similar to the one in question, opens it, pretends to read it, and then places it in close juxtaposition to the other. Again he converses, for some fifteen minutes, upon the public affairs. At length, in taking leave, he takes also from the table the letter to which he had no claim. Its rightful owner saw, but, of course, dared not call attention to the act, in the presence of the third personage who stood at her elbow. The minister decamped; leaving his own letter—one of no importance—upon the table." "Here, then," said Dupin to me, "you have precisely what you demand to make the ascendancy complete—the robber's knowledge of the loser's knowledge of the robber." "Yes," replied the Prefect; "and the power thus attained has, for some months past, been wielded, for political purposes, to a very dangerous extent. The personage robbed is more thoroughly convinced, every day, of the necessity of reclaiming her letter. But this, of course, cannot be done openly. In fine, driven to despair, she has committed the matter to me."

"Than whom," said Dupin, amid a perfect whirlwind of smoke, "no more sagacious agent could, I suppose, be desired, or even imagined." "You flatter me," replied the Prefect; "but it is possible that some such opinion may have been entertained." "It is clear," said I, "as you observe, that the letter is still in possession of the minister; since it is this possession, and not any employment of the letter, which bestows the power. With the employment the power departs."

"True," said G.; "and upon this conviction I proceeded. My first care was to make thorough search of the minister's hotel; and here my chief embarrassment lay in the necessity of searching without his knowledge. Beyond all things, I have been warned of the danger which would result from giving him reason to suspect our design." "But," said I, "you are quite au fait in these investigations. The Parisian police have done this thing often before." "O yes; and for this reason I did not despair. The habits of the minister gave me, too, a great advantage. He is frequently absent from home all night. His servants are by no means numerous. They sleep at a distance from their master's apartment, and, being chiefly Neapolitans, are readily made drunk. I have keys, as you know, with which I can open any chamber or cabinet in Paris. For three months a night has not passed, during the greater part of which I have not been engaged, personally, in ransacking the D— Hotel. My honor is interested, and, to mention a great secret, the reward is enormous. So I did not abandon the search until I had become fully satisfied that the thief is a more astute man than myself. I fancy that I have investigated every nook and corner of the premises in which it is possible that the paper can be concealed." "But is it not possible," I suggested, "that although the letter may be in possession of the minister, as it unquestionably is, he may have concealed it elsewhere than upon his own premises?" "This is barely possible," said Dupin. "The present peculiar condition of affairs at court, and especially of those intrigues in which D— is known to be involved, would render the instant availability of the document—its susceptibility of being produced at a moment's notice—a point of nearly equal importance with its possession."

"Its susceptibility of being produced?" said I. "That is to say, of being destroyed," said Dupin. "True," I observed; "the paper is clearly then upon the premises. As for its being upon the person of the minister, we may consider that as out of the question."

"Entirely," said the Prefect. "He has been twice waylaid, as if by footpads, and his person rigorously searched under my own inspection."

"You might have spared yourself this trouble," said Dupin. "D—, I presume, is not altogether a fool, and, if not, must have anticipated these waylayings, as a matter of course." "Not altogether a fool," said G., "but then he's a poet, which I take to be only one remove from a fool." "True," said Dupin, after a long and thoughtful whiff from his meerschaum, "although I have been guilty of certain doggrel myself."

"Suppose you detail," said I, "the particulars of your search."

"Why the fact is, we took our time, and we searched every where. I have had long experience in these affairs. I took the entire building, room by room; devoting the nights of a whole week to each. We examined, first, the furniture of each apartment. We opened every possible drawer; and I presume you know that, to a properly trained police agent, such a thing as a secret drawer is impossible. Any man is a dolt who permits a 'secret' drawer to escape him in a search of this kind. The thing is so plain. There is a certain amount of bulk—of space—to be accounted for in every cabinet. Then we have accurate rules. The fiftieth part of a line could not escape us. After the cabinets we took the chairs. The cushions we probed with the fine long needles you have seen me employ. From the tables we removed the tops."

"Why so?"

"Sometimes the top of a table, or other similarly arranged piece of furniture, is removed by the person wishing to conceal an article; then the leg is excavated, the article deposited within the cavity, and the top replaced. The bottoms and tops of bedposts are employed in the same way."

"But could not the cavity be detected by sounding?" I asked. "By no means, if, when the article is deposited, a sufficient wadding of cotton be placed around it. Besides, in our case, we were obliged to proceed without noise."

The Purloined Letteer

"But you could not have removed—you could not have taken to pieces all articles of furniture in which it would have been possible to make a deposit in the manner you mention. A letter may be compressed into a thin spiral roll, not differing much in shape or bulk from a large knitting-needle, and in this form it might be inserted into the rung of a chair, for example. You did not take to pieces all the chairs?"

"Certainly not; but we did better—we examined the rungs of every chair in the hotel, and, indeed the jointings of every description of furniture, by the aid of a most powerful microscope. Had there been any traces of recent disturbance we should not have failed to detect it instantly. A single grain of gimlet-dust, for example, would have been as obvious as an apple. Any disorder in the glueing—any unusual gaping in the joints—would have sufficed to insure detection." "I presume you looked to the mirrors, between the boards and the plates, and you probed the beds and the bed-clothes, as well as the curtains and carpets."

"That of course; and when we had absolutely completed every particle of the furniture in this way, then we examined the house itself. We divided its entire surface into compartments, which we numbered, so that none might be missed; then we scrutinized each individual square inch throughout the premises, including the two houses immediately adjoining, with the microscope, as before."

"The two houses adjoining!" I exclaimed; "you must have had a great deal of trouble."

"We had; but the reward offered is prodigious!" "You include the grounds about the houses?" "All the grounds are paved with brick. They gave us comparatively little trouble. We examined the moss between the bricks, and found it undisturbed."

"You looked among D—'s papers, of course, and into the books of the library?"

"Certainly; we opened every package and parcel; we not only opened every book, but we turned over every leaf in each volume, not contenting ourselves with a mere shake, according to the fashion of some of our police officers. We also measured the thickness of every book-cover, with the most accurate admeasurement, and applied to each the most jealous scrutiny of the microscope. Had any of the bindings been recently meddled with, it would have been utterly impossible that the fact should have escaped observation. Some five or six volumes, just from the hands of the binder, we carefully probed, longitudinally, with the needles."

"You explored the floors beneath the carpets?"

"Beyond doubt. We removed every carpet, and examined the boards with the microscope."

"And the paper on the walls?" "Yes."

"You looked into the cellars?" "We did."

"Then," I said, "you have been making a miscalculation, and the letter is not upon the premises, as you suppose."

"I fear you are right there," said the Prefect.

"And now, Dupin, what would you advise me to do?"

"To make a thorough re-search of the premises."

"That is absolutely needless," replied G—.

"I am not more sure that I breathe than I am that the letter is not at the Hotel."

"I have no better advice to give you," said Dupin. "You have, of course, an accurate description of the letter?"

"Oh yes!"—And here the Prefect, producing a memorandum-book proceeded to read aloud a minute account of the internal, and especially of the external appearance of the missing document. Soon after finishing the perusal of this description, he took his departure, more entirely depressed in spirits than I had ever known the good gentleman before. In about a month afterwards he paid us another visit, and found us occupied very nearly as before. He took a pipe and a chair and entered into some ordinary conversation. At length I said,—

"Well, but G—, what of the purloined letter? I presume you have at last made up your mind that there is no such thing as overreaching the Minister?"

"Confound him, say I—yes; I made the re-examination, however, as Dupin suggested—but it was all labor lost, as I knew it would be."

"How much was the reward offered, did you say?" asked Dupin.

"Why, a very great deal—a very liberal reward—I don't like to say how much, precisely; but one thing I will say, that I wouldn't mind giving my individual check for fifty thousand francs to any one who could obtain me that letter. The fact is, it is becoming of more and more importance every day; and the reward has been lately doubled. If it were trebled, however, I could do no more than I have done."

"Why, yes," said Dupin, drawlingly, between the whiffs of his meerschaum, "I really—think, G—, you have not exerted yourself—to the utmost in this matter. You might—do a little more, I think, eh?"

"How?—in what way?'

"Why—puff, puff—you might—puff, puff—employ counsel in the matter, eh?—puff, puff, puff. Do you remember the story they tell of Abernethy?"

"No; hang Abernethy!"

"To be sure! hang him and welcome. But, once upon a time, a certain rich miser conceived the design of spunging upon this Abernethy for a medical opinion. Getting up, for this purpose, an ordinary conversation in a private company, he insinuated his case to the physician, as that of an imaginary individual. " 'We will suppose,' said the miser, 'that his symptoms are such and such; now, doctor, what would you have directed him to take?' " 'Take!' said Abernethy, 'why, take advice, to be sure.' " "But," said the Prefect, a little discomposed, "I am perfectly willing to take advice, and to pay for it. I would really give fifty thousand francs to any one who would aid me in the matter." "In that case," replied Dupin, opening a drawer, and producing a check-book, "you may as well fill me up a check for the amount mentioned. When you have signed it, I will hand you the letter." I was astounded. The Prefect appeared absolutely thunder-stricken. For some minutes he remained speechless and motionless, looking incredulously at my friend with open mouth, and eyes that seemed starting from their sockets; then, apparently recovering himself in some measure, he seized a pen, and after several pauses and vacant stares, finally filled up and signed a check for fifty thousand francs, and handed it across the table to Dupin. The latter examined it carefully and deposited it in his pocket-book; then, unlocking an escritoire, took thence a letter and gave it to the Prefect. This functionary grasped it in a perfect agony of joy, opened it with a trembling hand, cast a rapid glance at its contents, and then, scrambling and struggling to the door, rushed at length unceremoniously from the room and from the house, without having uttered a syllable since Dupin had requested him to fill up the check.

When he had gone, my friend entered into some explanations. "The Parisian police," he said, "are exceedingly able in their way. They are persevering, ingenious, cunning, and thoroughly versed in the knowledge which their duties seem chiefly to demand. Thus, when G— detailed to us his made of searching the premises at the Hotel D—, I felt entire confidence in his having made a satisfactory investigation—so far as his labors extended." "So far as his labors extended?" said I. "Yes," said Dupin. "The measures adopted were not only the best of their kind, but carried out to absolute perfection. Had the letter been deposited within the range of their search, these fellows would, beyond a question, have found it." I merely laughed—but he seemed quite serious in all that he said. "The measures, then," he continued, "were good in their kind, and well executed; their defect lay in their being inapplicable to the case, and to the man. A certain set of highly ingenious resources are, with the Prefect, a sort of Procrustean bed, to which he forcibly adapts his designs. But he perpetually errs by being too deep or too shallow, for the matter in hand; and many a schoolboy is a better reasoner than he. I knew one about eight years of age, whose success at guessing in the game of 'even and odd' attracted universal admiration. This game is simple, and is played with marbles. One player holds in his hand a number of these toys, and demands of another whether that number is even or odd. If the guess is right, the guesser wins one; if wrong, he loses one. The boy to whom I allude won all the marbles of the school. Of course he had some principle of guessing; and this lay in mere observation and admeasurement of the astuteness of his opponents. For example, an arrant simpleton is his opponent, and, holding up his closed hand, asks, 'are they even or odd?' Our schoolboy replies, 'odd,' and loses; but upon the second trial he wins, for he then says to himself, 'the simpleton had them even upon the first trial, and his amount of cunning is just sufficient to make him have them odd upon the second; I will therefore guess odd;'—he guesses odd, and wins. Now, with a simpleton a degree above the first, he would have reasoned thus: 'This fellow finds that in the first instance I guessed odd, and, in the second, he will propose to himself, upon the first impulse, a simple variation from even to odd, as did the first simpleton; but then a second thought will suggest that this is too simple a variation, and finally he will decide upon putting it even as before. I will therefore guess even;'—he guesses even, and wins. Now this mode of reasoning in the schoolboy, whom his fellows termed 'lucky,'—what, in its last analysis, is it?" "It is merely," I said, "an identification of the reasoner's intellect with that of his opponent." "It is," said Dupin; "and, upon inquiring, of the boy by what means he effected the thorough identification in which his success consisted, I received answer as follows: 'When I wish to find out how wise, or how stupid, or how good, or how wicked is any one, or what are his thoughts at the moment, I fashion the expression of my face, as accurately as possible, in accordance with the expression of his, and then wait to see what thoughts or sentiments arise in my mind or heart, as if to match or correspond with the expression.' This response of the schoolboy lies at the bottom of all the spurious profundity which has been attributed to Rochefoucault, to La Bougive, to Machiavelli, and to Campanella." "And the identification," I said, "of the reasoner's intellect with that of his opponent, depends, if I understand you aright, upon the accuracy with which the opponent's intellect is admeasured." "For its practical value it depends upon this," replied Dupin; "and the Prefect and his cohort fail so frequently, first, by default of this identification, and, secondly, by ill-admeasurement, or rather through non-admeasurement, of the intellect with which they are engaged. They consider only their own ideas of ingenuity; and, in searching for anything hidden, advert only to the modes in which they would have hidden it. They are right in this much—that their own ingenuity is a faithful representative of that of the mass; but when the cunning of the individual felon is diverse in character from their own, the felon foils them, of course. This always happens when it is above their own, and very usually when it is below. They have no variation of principle in their investigations; at best, when urged by some unusual emergency—by some extraordinary reward—they extend or exaggerate their old modes of practice, without touching their principles. What, for example, in this case of D—, has been done to vary the principle of action? What is all this boring, and probing, and sounding, and scrutinizing with the microscope and dividing the surface of the building into registered square inches—what is it all but an exaggeration of the application of the one principle or set of principles of search, which are based upon the one set of notions regarding human ingenuity, to which the Prefect, in the long routine of his duty, has been accustomed? Do you not see he has taken it for granted that all men proceed to conceal a letter,—not exactly in a gimlet hole bored in a chair-leg—but, at least, in some out-of-the-way hole or corner suggested by the same tenor of thought which would urge a man to secrete a letter in a gimlet-hole bored in a chair-leg? And do you not see also, that such recherchès nooks for concealment are adapted only for ordinary occasions, and would be adopted only by ordinary intellects; for, in all cases of concealment, a disposal of the article concealed—a disposal of it in this recherchè manner,—is, in the very first instance, presumable and presumed; and thus its discovery depends, not at all upon the acumen, but altogether upon the mere care, patience, and determination of the seekers; and where the case is of importance—or, what amounts to the same thing in the policial eyes, when the reward is of magnitude,—the qualities in question have never been known to fail. You will now understand what I meant in suggesting that, had the purloined letter been hidden any where within the limits of the Prefect's examination—in other words, had the principle of its concealment been comprehended within the principles of the Prefect—its discovery would have been a matter altogether beyond question. This functionary, however, has been thoroughly mystified; and the remote source of his defeat lies in the supposition that the Minister is a fool, because he has acquired renown as a poet. All fools are poets; this the Prefect feels; and he is merely guilty of a *non distributio medii* in thence inferring that all poets are fools."

"But is this really the poet?" I asked. "There are two brothers, I know; and both have attained reputation in letters. The Minister I believe has written learnedly on the Differential Calculus. He is a mathematician, and no poet."

"You are mistaken; I know him well; he is both. As poet and mathematician, he would reason well; as mere mathematician, he could not have reasoned at all, and thus would have been at the mercy of the Prefect."

"You surprise me," I said, "by these opinions, which have been contradicted by the voice of the world. You do not mean to set at naught the well-digested idea of centuries. The mathematical reason has long been regarded as the reason par excellence." " '*Il y a à parièr*,' " replied Dupin, quoting from Chamfort, " '*que toute idèe publique, toute convention reçue est une sottise, car elle a convenue au plus grand nombre*.' The mathematicians, I grant you, have done their best to promulgate the popular error to which you allude, and which is none the less an error for its promulgation as truth. With an art worthy a better cause, for example, they have insinuated the term 'analysis' into application to algebra. The French are the originators of this particular deception; but if a term is of any importance—if words derive any value from applicability—then 'analysis' conveys 'algebra' about as much as, in Latin, 'ambitus' implies 'ambition,' 'religio' 'religion,' or 'homines honesti,' a set of honorablemen." "You have a quarrel on hand, I see," said I, "with some of the algebraists of Paris; but proceed." "I dispute the availability, and thus the value, of that reason which is cultivated in any especial form other than the abstractly logical. I dispute, in particular, the reason educed by mathematical study. The mathematics are the science of form and quantity; mathematical reasoning is merely logic applied to observation upon form and quantity. The great error lies in supposing that even the truths of what is called pure algebra, are abstract or general truths. And this error is so egregious that I am confounded at the universality with which it has been received. Mathematical axioms are not axioms of general truth. What is true of relation—of form and quantity—is often grossly false in regard to morals, for example. In this latter science it is very usually untrue that the aggregated parts are equal to the whole. In chemistry also the axiom fails. In the consideration of motive it fails; for two motives, each of a given value, have not, necessarily, a value when united, equal to the sum of their values apart. There are numerous other mathematical truths which are only truths within the limits of relation. But the mathematician argues, from his finite truths, through habit, as if they were of an absolutely general applicability—as the world indeed imagines them to be. Bryant, in his very learned 'Mythology,' mentions an analogous source of error, when he says that 'although the Pagan fables are not believed, yet we forget ourselves continually, and make inferences from them as existing realities.' With the algebraists, however, who are Pagans themselves, the 'Pagan fables' are believed, and the inferences are made, not so much through lapse of memory, as through an unaccountable addling of the brains. In short, I never yet encountered the mere mathematician who could be trusted out of equal roots, or one who did not clandestinely hold it as a point of his faith that x2+px was absolutely and unconditionally equal to q. Say to one of these gentlemen, by way of experiment, if you please, that you believe occasions may occur where x2+px is not altogether equal to q, and, having made him understand what you mean, get out of his reach as speedily as convenient, for, beyond doubt, he will endeavor to knock you down.

"I mean to say," continued Dupin, while I merely laughed at his last observations, "that if the Minister had been no more than a mathematician, the Prefect would have been under no necessity of giving me this check. I know him, however, as both mathematician and poet, and my measures were adapted to his capacity, with reference to the circumstances by which he was surrounded. I knew him as a courtier, too, and as a bold intriguant. Such a man, I considered, could not fail to be aware of the ordinary policial modes of action. He could not have failed to anticipate—and events have proved that he did not fail to anticipate—the waylayings to which he was subjected. He must have foreseen, I reflected, the secret investigations of his premises. His frequent absences from home at night, which were hailed by the Prefect as certain aids to his success, I regarded only as ruses, to afford opportunity for thorough search to the police, and thus the sooner to impress them with the conviction to which G—, in fact, did finally arrive—the conviction that the letter was not upon the premises. I felt, also, that the whole train of thought, which I was at some pains in detailing to you just now, concerning the invariable principle of policial action in searches for articles concealed—I felt that this whole train of thought would necessarily pass through the mind of the Minister. It would imperatively lead him to despise all the ordinary nooks of concealment. He could not, I reflected, be so weak as not to see that the most intricate and remote recess of his hotel would be as open as his commonest closets to the eyes, to the probes, to the gimlets, and to the microscopes of the Prefect. I saw, in fine, that he would be driven, as a matter of course, to simplicity, if not deliberately induced to it as a matter of choice. You will remember, perhaps, how desperately the Prefect laughed when I suggested, upon our first interview, that it was just possible this mystery troubled him so much on account of its being so very self-evident." "Yes," said I, "I remember his merriment well. I really thought he would have fallen into convulsions." "The material world," continued Dupin, "abounds with very strict analogies to the immaterial; and thus some color of truth has been given to the rhetorical dogma, that metaphor, or simile, may be made to strengthen an argument, as well as to embellish a description. The principle of the *vis inertiæ*, for example, seems to be identical in physics and metaphysics. It is not more true in the former, that a large body is with more difficulty set in motion than a smaller one, and that its subsequent momentum is commensurate with this difficulty, than it is, in the latter, that intellects of the vaster capacity, while more forcible, more constant, and more eventful in their movements than those of inferior grade, are yet the less readily moved, and more embarrassed and full of hesitation in the first few steps of their progress. Again: have you ever noticed which of the street signs, over the shop-doors, are the most attractive of attention?"

"I have never given the matter a thought," I said. "There is a game of puzzles," he resumed, "which is played upon a map. One party playing requires another to find a given word—the name of town, river, state or empire—any word, in short, upon the motley and perplexed surface of the chart. A novice in the game generally seeks to embarrass his opponents by giving them the most minutely lettered names; but the adept selects such words as stretch, in large characters, from one end of the chart to the other. These, like the over-largely lettered signs and placards of the street, escape observation by dint of being excessively obvious; and here the physical oversight is precisely analogous with the moral inapprehension by which the intellect suffers to pass unnoticed those considerations which are too obtrusively and too palpably self-evident. But this is a point, it appears, somewhat above or beneath the understanding of the Prefect. He never once thought it probable, or possible, that the Minister had deposited the letter immediately beneath the nose of the whole world, by way of best preventing any portion of that world from perceiving it. "But the more I reflected upon the daring, dashing, and discriminating ingenuity of D—; upon the fact that the document must always have been at hand, if he intended to use it to good purpose; and upon the decisive evidence, obtained by the Prefect, that it was not hidden within the limits of that dignitary's ordinary search—the more satisfied I became that, to conceal this letter, the Minister had resorted to the comprehensive and sagacious expedient of not attempting to conceal it at all.

"Full of these ideas, I prepared myself with a pair of green spectacles, and called one fine morning, quite by accident, at the Ministerial hotel. I found D— at home, yawning, lounging, and dawdling, as usual, and pretending to be in the last extremity of ennui. He is, perhaps, the most really energetic human being now alive—but that is only when nobody sees him. "To be even with him, I complained of my weak eyes, and lamented the necessity of the spectacles, under cover of which I cautiously and thoroughly surveyed the whole apartment, while seemingly intent only upon the conversation of my host.

"I paid especial attention to a large writing-table near which he sat, and upon which lay confusedly, some miscellaneous letters and other papers, with one or two musical instruments and a few books. Here, however, after a long and very deliberate scrutiny, I saw nothing to excite particular suspicion.

"At length my eyes, in going the circuit of the room, fell upon a trumpery fillagree card-rack of pasteboard, that hung dangling by a dirty blue ribbon, from a little brass knob just beneath the middle of the mantelpiece. In this rack, which had three or four compartments, were five or six visiting cards and a solitary letter. This last was much soiled and crumpled. It was torn nearly in two, across the middle—as if a design, in the first instance, to tear it entirely up as worthless, had been altered, or stayed, in the second. It had a large black seal, bearing the D— cipher very conspicuously, and was addressed, in a diminutive female hand, to D—, the minister, himself. It was thrust carelessly, and even, as it seemed, contemptuously, into one of the uppermost divisions of the rack.

"No sooner had I glanced at this letter, than I concluded it to be that of which I was in search. To be sure, it was, to all appearance, radically different from the one of which the Prefect had read us so minute a description. Here the seal was large and black, with the D— cipher; there it was small and red, with the ducal arms of the S— family. Here, the address, to the Minister, diminutive and feminine; there the superscription, to a certain royal personage, was markedly bold and decided; the size alone formed a point of correspondence. But, then, the radicalness of these differences, which was excessive; the dirt; the soiled and torn condition of the paper, so inconsistent with the true methodical habits of D—, and so suggestive of a design to delude the beholder into an idea of the worthlessness of the document; these things, together with the hyper-obtrusive situation of this document, full in the view of every visiter, and thus exactly in accordance with the conclusions to which I had previously arrived; these things, I say, were strongly corroborative of suspicion, in one who came with the intention to suspect.

"I protracted my visit as long as possible, and, while I maintained a most animated discussion with the Minister upon a topic which I knew well had never failed to interest and excite him, I kept my attention really riveted upon the letter. In this examination, I committed to memory its external appearance and arrangement in the rack; and also fell, at length, upon a discovery which set at rest whatever trivial doubt I might have entertained. In scrutinizing the edges of the paper, I observed them to be more chafed than seemed necessary. They presented the broken appearance which is manifested when a stiff paper, having been once folded and pressed with a folder, is refolded in a reversed direction, in the same creases or edges which had formed the original fold. This discovery was sufficient. It was clear to me that the letter had been turned, as a glove, inside out, re-directed, and re-sealed. I bade the Minister good morning, and took my departure at once, leaving a gold snuff-box upon the table.

"The next morning I called for the snuff-box, when we resumed, quite eagerly, the conversation of the preceding day. While thus engaged, however, a loud report, as if of a pistol, was heard immediately beneath the windows of the hotel, and was succeeded by a series of fearful screams, and the shoutings of a terrified mob. D— rushed to a casement, threw it open, and looked out. In the meantime, I stepped to the card-rack took the letter, put it in my pocket, and replaced it by a fac-simile, (so far as regards externals,) which I had carefully prepared at my lodgings—imitating the D— cipher, very readily, by means of a seal formed of bread. "The disturbance in the street had been occasioned by the frantic behavior of a man with a musket. He had fired it among a crowd of women and children. It proved, however, to have been without ball, and the fellow was suffered to go his way as a lunatic or a drunkard. When he had gone,

D— came from the window, whither I had followed him immediately upon securing the object in view. Soon afterwards I bade him farewell. The pretended lunatic was a man in my own pay." "But what purpose had you," I asked, "in replacing the letter by a fac-simile? Would it not have been better, at the first visit, to have seized it openly, and departed?" "D—," replied Dupin, "is a desperate man, and a man of nerve. His hotel, too, is not without attendants devoted to his interests. Had I made the wild attempt you suggest, I might never have left the Ministerial presence alive. The good people of Paris might have heard of me no more. But I had an object apart from these considerations. You know my political prepossessions. In this matter, I act as a partisan of the lady concerned. For eighteen months the Minister has had her in his power. She has now him in hers—since, being unaware that the letter is not in his possession, he will proceed with his exactions as if it was. Thus will he inevitably commit himself, at once, to his political destruction. His downfall, too, will not be more precipitate than awkward. It is all very well to talk about the facilis descensus Averni; but in all kinds of climbing, as Catalani said of singing, it is far more easy to get up than to come down. In the present instance I have no sympathy—at least no pity—for him who descends. He is that monstrum horrendum, an unprincipled man of genius. I confess, however, that I should like very well to know the precise character of his thoughts, when, being defied by her whom the Prefect terms 'a certain personage' he is reduced to opening the letter which I left for him in the card-rack."

"How? did you put any thing particular in it?"

"Why—it did not seem altogether right to leave the interior blank—that would have been insulting. D—, at Vienna once, did me an evil turn, which I told him, quite good-humoredly, that I should remember. So, as I knew he would feel some curiosity in regard to the identity of the person who had outwitted him, I thought it a pity not to give him a clue. He is well acquainted with my MS., and I just copied into the middle of the blank sheet the words—" '——*Un dessein si funeste, S'il n'est digne d'Atrèe, est digne de Thyeste.*

They are to be found in Crebillon's 'Atrèe.'"

The Purloined Letteer

About the Author:

Edgar Allan Poe (1809–1849) was an iconic American writer, poet, and literary critic, widely regarded as a pioneer of Gothic literature and the short story form. Renowned for his tales of mystery and macabre, Poe's works delve into themes of death, madness, and the supernatural, often blending psychological depth with eerie, atmospheric settings.

Poe's works often explore themes of death, madness, obsession, and the macabre, characteristics that define the Gothic tradition. Gothic fiction, which emerged in the late 18th century, combines elements of horror, mystery, and romance, typically set against eerie, oppressive, and often decaying backdrops.

Poe's works helped define the genre, particularly through his exploration of the psychological states of his characters. His stories often deal with internal turmoil, the descent into madness, and the supernatural, blurring the line between reality and nightmare.

Some of his most famous works include *The Raven* (a haunting poem), *The Tell-Tale Heart*, *The Fall of the House of Usher*, and *The Cask of Amontillado*. Poe is also credited with creating the modern detective story, as seen in *The Murders in the Rue Morgue.*

Introduction:

Of all of Poe's stories of ratiocination (or detective stories), "The Purloined Letter" is considered his finest. This is partially due to the fact that there are no gothic elements, such as the gruesome descriptions of dead bodies, as there was in "The Murders in the Rue Morgue." But more important, this is the story that employs most effectively the principle of ratiocination; this story brilliantly illustrates the concept of the intuitive intellect at work as it solves a problem logically. Finally, more than with most of his stories, this one is told with utmost economy.

"The Purloined Letter" emphasizes several devices from "The Murders in the Rue Morgue" and adds several others.

The story is divided into two parts. In the first part, Monsieur G , Prefect of Police in Paris, visits Dupin with a problem: A letter has been stolen and is being used to blackmail the person from whom it was stolen. The thief is known (Minister D) and the method is known (substitution viewed by the victim, who dared not protest). The problem is to retrieve the letter, since the writer and the victim, as well as Minister D , have important posts in the government; the demands he is making are becoming dangerous politically. The Prefect has searched Minister D 's home thoroughly, even taking the furniture apart; he and his men have found nothing. Dupin's advice is that they thoroughly re-search the house. A month later, Monsieur G returns, having found nothing. This time, he says that he will pay fifty thousand francs to anyone who can obtain the letter for him. Dupin invites him to write the check; when this is done, Dupin hands the Prefect the letter without any further comment.

The second half of "The Purloined Letter" consists of Dupin's explanation, to his chronicler, of how he obtained the letter. One of his basic assumptions is an inversion of one of the aphorisms that was introduced in "The Murders in the Rue Morgue"; the case is so difficult to solve because it appears to be so simple. Beyond that, Dupin introduces the method of psychological deduction. Before he did anything else, he reviewed everything he knew about Minister D. Then, he reviewed what he knew about the case. With this in mind, Dupin tried to reconstruct the Minister's thinking, deciding that he would very likely have hidden the letter in plain sight. Using this theory, Dupin visited MinisterD and found the letter in plain sight but boldly disguised. He memorized the appearance of the letter, and he left a snuffbox as an excuse to return. Having duplicated the letter, he exchanged his facsimile for the original during a prearranged diversion. Retrieving his snuff-box, he departed. His solution introduces into detective fiction the formula of "the most obvious place."

Dupin is, of course, the original eccentric but brilliant detective. He seems to be a very private person, though one with connections and acquaintances in many places. He prefers the darkness and the evening; darkness, he feels, is particularly conducive to reflection. He prefers to gather his information and to ponder thoroughly before any action is taken. He talks little; an hour or more of contemplative silence seems common. And, of course, he is an expert in the psychology of people of various types; indeed, he seems to be learned in a number of areas — mathematics and poetry, for example.

The Prefect, Monsieur G, is a contrast to Dupin. Whereas Dupin is primarily concerned with the psychological elements of the case, G is almost wholly concerned with physical details and evidence. G talks much and says little. Dupin considers things broadly, while G 's point of view is extremely narrow. Anything G does not understand is "odd" and not worth considering; for Dupin, that is a matter for investigation. G believes in a great deal of physical activity during an investigation, while Dupin believes in a maximum of thought and a minimum of physical exertion. Though Dupin says that the Paris police are excellent within their limitations, it is clear that G 's limitations are quite severe.

The personality of the unnamed narrator, the Dupin-chronicler, lies between these two extremes. Though he shares some of Dupin's tastes silent contemplation in darkness, for example and has some understanding of Dupin's methods, he seems psychologically closer to G than to Dupin. He seems to be a rather ordinary person with rather ordinary views and ideas. Thus, his assumptions and his interjections are often erroneous; he assumes, for example, that if the police have not been able to find the letter after their search, then it must be elsewhere. In his argument with Dupin about mathematicians, the narrator takes the common view and attitude toward mathematicians, a position that Dupin explicitly suggests is idiocy. In other words, the narrator is a mediator between Dupin and the reader. His reactions are similar to those of the reader, though he is somewhat less astute than the reader, so that the reader can feel superior to him. Naturally, such a narrator guides our attitudes toward Dupin, G , and the case. He is, for example, in awe of Dupin's abilities and methods; while the reader may maintain a more critical distance, he is guided in that direction to some degree. Finally, such a narrator determines the amount of information which a reader receives and guides the attention of the reader to the information received. In this case, the narrator tells us everything, but only as he receives it; because he did not witness the case being solved, the reader doesn't either.

The idea that the reader is a participant in the investigation of a crime and thus should be given all the information on which the detective bases his conclusions is quite modern. In "The Purloined Letter," the reader has little chance to participate, first because little information about Minister D 's character is given in the first half of the story, and, second, because there is no indication of any activity by Dupin until the second half. Poe's purpose was not to invite reader participation, but rather to emphasize rationality, stressing logical thinking as the means of solving problems. Consequently, Dupin's exposition of his thought processes are the most important part of the story. Without this highlighting of the logical investigation and solution of a problem, the detective story may never have developed; it would certainly be very different if it had. However, with this method and approach established, it became logical, and rather easy, to evolve the idea of the reader as a participant.

Attempting to determine the psychology of the criminal is an honorable tradition in detective fiction. The particular methods that are used change as more is learned about human beings, their behaviors, and their motivations; they also change, perhaps even more, as psychological theories change. Thus, much of Poe's — or Dupin's psychology, especially the explanations, seems dated. For instance, the boy whom Dupin uses as an example arranges his face so it is as similar to the other person's expression as possible; this is supposed to give rise to thoughts and feelings that are similar to those of the other person. In the sense that outward expressions facial expressions, clothes, and so on — are thought to influence the way a person feels, this idea is somewhat still current; however, that effect is thought to be general rather than specific, and we no longer believe that we can gain much knowledge of another person in this way. In addition, it is probably true that certain habits of thinking are likely to contribute to a person's success in a field; however, the distinctions are by no means as rigid as Poe made them seem, nor are the qualities so narrow. Although the principles that Dupin works from are rather outdated, his method is direct. This method is, of course, applicable to other kinds of problems posed in detective fiction; whenever the detective can learn and apply some knowledge of the criminal's psychology, he is closer to the solution of the crime.

Other details in "The Purloined Letter" reveal the story's era and the political system in France, Dupin's comments about poetry, mathematics, and the sciences in particular. Nevertheless, the story still reads well, and the details are overshadowed by the sweep of the puzzle and the story. Even if the story were not still interesting reading, "The Purloined Letter" would be of prime historical importance for it establishes the method of psychological deduction, the solution of the most obvious place, and the assumption that the case that seems simplest may be the most difficult to solve. Also it gives importance on keeping things safe will keep the problems away. Whether one is interested in good reading or has a historical interest in detective fiction, "The Purloined Letter" provides both.

Glossary

1. Purloined: Stolen or taken dishonestly.
2. Epistle: A letter or written communication, often formal or literary.
3. Acumen: The ability to make quick, accurate judgments
4. Sagacity: Wisdom or keen mental discernment
5. Hypothesis: A proposed explanation made on the basis of limited evidence
6. Ratiocination: The process of logical reasoning, a hallmark.
7. Conspicuous: Easily seen or noticed
8. Espionage: The practice of spying or using spies to obtain secret information
9. Superfluities: Excess or unnecessary items
10. Adroitness: Skill or cleverness in using the hands or mind
11. Conjecture: An opinion or conclusion formed on the basis of incomplete information,

12. Impertinence: Lack of respect or rudeness
13. Subterfuge: Deceit used to achieve one's goals
14. Pecuniary: Relating to money
15. Inordinate: Exceeding reasonable limits

Choose the correct answer

1. Who is the narrator of The Purloined Letter?

a) C. Auguste Dupin b) Dupin's friend c) The Prefect of Police d) Minister D

2. What crime is at the center of The Purloined Letter?

a) A robbery b) A murder c) A theft of a compromising letter d) A forgery

3. Who initially investigates the theft of the letter?

a) The narrator b) C. Auguste Dupin c) The Prefect of Police d) Minister D

4. Who is the primary suspect in the theft of the letter?

a) The Prefect b) Minister D c) The narrator d) Dupin

5. Why does the Prefect fail to find the letter during his search of the suspect's house?

a) He does not search thoroughly.

b) Minister D outsmarts him by hiding the letter in plain sight.

c) The letter is not in the house.

d) The Prefect is bribed.

6. What is Dupin's key insight into solving the case?

a) The letter is hidden in an elaborate secret compartment.

b) The criminal has disguised the letter as something ordinary.

c) The letter was destroyed.

d) The Prefect already has the letter but does not realize it.

7. How does Dupin recover the purloined letter?

a) By searching the house himself

b) By bribing a servant of Minister D

c) By staging a distraction and replacing the letter with a fake

d) By convincing Minister D to hand it over

8. What is Dupin's motive for helping the Prefect solve the case?

a) for justice b) Financial reward c) Revenge on Minister D d) To outwit the Prefect

9. How does Dupin view Minister D?

a) As criminal genius b) As incompetent person c) As an ally d) As a tragic figure

10. What literary device is most prominent in The Purloined Letter?

a) Foreshadowing b) Irony c) Allegory d) Symbolism

11. Edgar Allan Poe is best known for his contributions to which literary genre?

a). Romantic poetry b). Gothic fiction c). Historical fiction d). Science fiction

12. What is the name of Poe's only completed novel?

a) The Gold-Bug b)The Narrative of Arthur Gordon Pym of Nantucket

c) The Purloined Letter d) The Black Cat

13. . "The Purloined Letter" is one of the early classics of American literature and it is one of the United States' first mystery stories. In what year was this classic by Edgar Allan Poe first published?

a) 1840 b)1844 c)1950 d)1820

14. What is the significance of the purloined letter?

a) It contains a treasure map.

b) It holds evidence of a political conspiracy.

c) It has incriminating information about a royal person.

d) It is a love letter.

MR. KNOW ALL
-WILLIAM SOMERSET MAUGHAM

About the author

William Somerset Maugham is a 20th century short story writer, novelist and playwright. He wrote the story 'Mr. Know All' in the year 1966. The story is a brilliant read and concentrates of racial prejudice and stereotypes. It also tells people that looks can be deceiving, which is why we should not jump on to make opinions about people. On the other hand, the other side of the coin is that one should make impressive first impressions instead of the ones that can make people around uncomfortable.

His works are known for their insight into human nature, their exploration of complex moral and psychological themes, and their vivid depictions of settings and characters. Maugham's writing is often characterized by its straightforward prose style, wit, and a focus on human relationships, especially in the face of life's challenges. Maugham's writing career began with short stories, but he quickly became known for his novels, plays, and short story collections. His works often examined the lives of ordinary people, particularly the complexities of their relationships, desires, and moral dilemmas.

Characters

There are four main characters in the story:

- Mr. Max Keleda: A self-proclaimed Englishman, but who is called a Levantine and Mr. Know all. Mr. Keleda has a dark complexion and curly hair, due to which he does not look English to the narrator.
- The Narrator: An unknown man who is on a 14 days voyage with Mr. Keleda. He also shares a cabin with him.

- Mr. Ramsay: An overconfident and argumentative person who is travelling with his wife to Japan. He is the only person on the ship who matches the antics of Mr. Keleda
- Mrs. Ramsay: Mr. Ramsay's wife whose pearl necklace leads to the main conflict in the story.

Introduction of Two Main Characters

The story begins with the narrator explaining the readers how difficult it was to find an accommodation on the ship, which was travelling from San Francisco to Yokohama and the time was soon after the end of World War 2. The narrator was lucky to find a cabin with only two berths. However, he got sad to find out that his traveling partner is not of a Western descent. In the beginning only, the narrator had shown his disgust towards non-English people when he said he would have preferred a partner named Smith or Brown. This shows the existing racism and prejudice in the narrator's mind.

The narrator has already described how untidy and unkept Mr. Keleda was. His stuff was unpacked and lying all around the cabin. Soon, he also meets Mr. Keleda in the smoking room.

Mr. Keleda's Nature

In contrary to the narrator's character, Mr. Keleda is an open and very emotional person. When he finds the narrator sitting alone in the smoking room and playing a game of cards, he abruptly starts a conversion. Even when the narrator wanted to finish the game of cards alone, Mr. Keleda helps him out. Later, Mr. Keleda also shows the narrator three magic tricks when he had clearly refused to see a single one. This shows how disrespectful Mr. Keleda is towards the decisions and feelings of other people. Due to this very exact nature, he becomes the most disliked person on the ship. He forces people to listen to his talks even when no wants to and pretends to know everything. This is a major flaw in Mr. Keleda's character.

Mr. Keleda's interfering nature

Mr. Keleda wants to take part in everyone's business. Basically, he sticks around everywhere and talks to everyone. On his own accord, he takes various responsibilities on the ship, including collecting prizes for sports, conducting auctions, concerts and even managing the ball room. He also likes to talk on multiple topics including politics, business, plays, pictures and even nationalism. Due to his over-talkative behavior, people mostly prefer to avoid him.

The Conflict

Mr. Know All Summary: This is the very important part of the story and also the most confusing for non-native English speakers. It is in this part of the story that the characters Mr. and Mrs. Ramsay are introduced. Mr. Ramsay is an American Counselor who works in Kobe, Japan. When he is in Japan, he leaves his wife at home in New York. Mr. Ramsay is the only stubborn and relentless person other than Mr. Keleda on the ship. One evening, when everybody is discussing about pearls, Mr. Ramsay and Mr. Keleda enter into a heated argument over Japanese pearls. The narrator knew that Ramsay had no expertise in pearls but he just wanted to irritate Mr. Keleda.

Mr. Ramsay is also successful in his efforts when Mr. Keleda had to burst out his profession of being a pearl trader. Keleda was in the business of pearls and diamonds, which he hadn't told to anyone on the ship prior to losing his cool in this argument. In the heat of the moment, he also blurts out while pointing a finger at Mrs. Ramsay's pearl necklace that even from this distance, he can tell that the pearls are high-quality, real and very expensive.

Now this is where the real conflict starts.

Mr. Ramsay places a bet of $100 on the pearl necklace with 100% confidence that the pearls are fake. He was told by his wife that she bought it for really cheap at a local department store. Being stubborn himself, Mr. Keleda accepts the bet. Mr. Ramsay on the other hand, takes out the necklace from his wife's neck and hands it over to Mr. Keleda. Mr. Keleda inspects the necklace carefully under a magnifying glass and realizes at an instant that the necklace is indeed 100% real and very costly. At this point, Mr. Keleda has almost won the bet. However, no sooner he got the chance to tell everyone, he caught the look on Mrs. Ramsay's face. She looked anxious and scared. Seeing that look, Mr. Keleda instantly realizes that the pearl necklace is actually given to her by her lover in New York. Mr. Ramsay is not aware of that and revealing this fact can break Mr. and Mrs. Ramsay's marriage.

Thus, to protect their marriage, Mr. Know-all accepts defeat and tells everyone that he was wrong, the necklace is fake. He also takes out a $100 note and gives it to Mr. Ramsay. Everyone insults Mr. Keleda and talks of his defeat spread across the ship. The next morning, somebody knocks at Mr. Keleda and the narrator's cabin, and slips an envelope inside. That envelope had $100 bill for Mr. Keleda. After this, Mr. Keleda tells the narrator everything. On realizing the heights to which Mr. Keleda went for protecting Ramsays' marriage, the narrator finally starts respecting Mr. Keleda.

Conclusion and Analysis

The story is a great example of how we should not judge someone by their appearance, as appearances can deceive.

Likewise, one should also respect the privacy and choices of others, or else that person only receives hatred in return. Although, he may have harmless intentions, but still can be misunderstood. Two other themes that we can see in the story are racism and adultery. The narrator often uses the word 'Levantine' as a slur to describe Mr. Keleda. Although, the word 'Levantine' only means someone from eastern-Mediterranean descent and is not a racial slur in the language, it is the way that the narrator uses it in the story, to sterortype Mr. Keleda that it can be interpreted in a racial way.

Lastly, Mr. Ramsay was a cunning but ignorant man who used to leave his beautiful wife in the US on his work trips to Japan. As a result, his wife fell in love with a guy from New York who also gifted her the pearl necklace that created the entire conflict. It was only for Mr. Keleda's selfless decision that Mr. and Mrs. Ramsay's marriage was saved.

Glossary

1. Ocean Liner: A large ship used for transporting people across seas
2. Oriental: A term historically used to describe people or things from Asia, particularly the Middle East and South Asia, though it is considered outdated and inappropriate today.
3. Chauvinistic: Having an exaggerated or aggressive patriotism or belief in the superiority of one's own group.
4. Patronizing: Acting superior and condescending toward others
5. Unprepossessing: Not particularly attractive or impressive in appearance

6. Dogmatic: Expressing opinions as if they are unquestionably correct
7. Demeanor: A person's outward behavior or manner
8. Affable: Friendly and easy to talk to
9. Opulent: Luxurious or wealthy
10. Deferential: Showing respect or submission to someone
11. Allof: Distant or reserved in manner; not friendly or forthcomin
12. Levity: Lack of seriousness, often in an inappropriate or disrespectful way.

Choose the correct Answer

1. Where does the story take place?

a) A hotel b) A small village c) A cruise ship d) A courtroom

2. What is Mr. Kelada's nationality?

a) British b) Indian c) American d) Middle Eastern

3. What is the narrator's initial impression of Mr. Kelada?

a) Polite & reserved b) Overbearing & loud c) Humble & modest d) Mysterious & secretive

4. What nickname is given to Mr. Kelada?

a) Know-All b) The Pearl Expert c) The Captain d) The Oriental Gentleman

5. What object is central to the main conflict of the story?

a) A ring b) A pearl necklace c) A diamond bracelet d) A gold watch

6. Who owns the pearl necklace that becomes a subject of debate?

a) Mrs. Ramsay b) Mr. Kelada c) The narrator d) The ship captain

7. How does Mr. Kelada react when he realizes the truth about the necklace?

a) He exposes Mrs. Ramsay's secret.

b) He pretends to be wrong about his judgment.

c) He angrily confronts Mr. Ramsay.

d) He leaves the ship in shame.

8. Why does Mr. Kelada choose to lose the bet?

a) To protect Mrs. Ramsay's reputation.

b) Because he realizes he was wrong.

c) To gain favor with the narrator.

d) Out of fear of Mr. Ramsay.

9. How does the narrator's opinion of Mr. Kelada change by the end of the story?

a) He continues to dislike him.

b) He starts to respect him.

c) He feels indifferent toward him.

d) He ridicules him even more.

10. What is the central theme of the story?

a) Cultural superiority

b) The importance of honesty

c) Appearances versus reality

d) The value of wealth

11. What is Mr. Kelada's profession?

a) A government clerk

b) A jeweler and gem expert

c) A travel agent

d) A businessman dealing in luxury goods

12. Why does the narrator's opinion of Mr. Know-All change?

a). He learns about Mr. Know-All's true identity.

b). He realizes Mr. Know-All has a kind heart.

c). He discovers Mr. Know-All's expertise.

d). He witnesses Mr. Know-All's act of bravery.

THE THIEF'S STORY
- RUSKIN BOND

About the Author:

Ruskin Bond is one of India's most cherished authors, known for his evocative storytelling and deep connection with nature and rural India. Born on May 19, 1934, in Kasauli, British India, Bond has authored numerous novels, short stories, and poems, often drawing inspiration from his life in the Himalayan foothills. His writing style is simple yet profound, capturing the innocence of childhood, the beauty of the mountains, and the nuances of human relationships. Some of his notable works include The Room on the Roof, Rusty, the Boy from the Hills, and The Blue Umbrella. Bond has received several accolades, including the Sahitya Akademi Award and the Padma Shri, for his contribution to Indian literature.

Summary and analysis:

The Thief Story is a short story was written by Ruskin Bond. A Thief and an innocent, kind-hearted man are depicted in The Thief Summary. It conveys a simple but meaningful message to society. It emphasizes human values and relationships. The quotation states that greedy people can bc robbed easily of their wealth, whereas honest and careless people are more difficult to defraud. That is exactly what the Story is about. In this Story, the boy constantly changes his name in order to avoid getting identified. As a result, he had few friends because he viewed them as troublesome. A summary of the Chapter the Thief Story informs us that Anil was the only man the Thief knew, who took him under his wing, taught him basic knowledge, and treated him as a brother. According to the summary of The Thief Story, Class 10, the main character, Hari Singh, plans and plots to rob the only person who cares for him.

His conscience prevents him from doing so. Despite being noticed, he returned the money without being noticed and was successful in his objective. Having good values in life will change a person's attitude towards life, according to the Thief Story summary.

The Thief's Story was written by Ruskin Bond. Throughout the Story, Hari Singh, a fifteen-year-old boy, befriends people in order to rob them. While competing in a wrestling match, he met Anil. It was the twenty-fifth year of Anil's life, and he was living a casual existence. In spite of his writing ability, he only managed to earn a small amount of money. As part of Hari's befriending effort, he asked Anil for some work. When Anil asked him if he could cook, the young boy replied with a yes. After hearing this, Anil took Hari to his room, promising to teach him how to read, write, add numbers, as well as how to prepare delicious meals. When Anil was feeling generous, he would give Hari a rupee as a tip. The other day, Anil received a bundle of notes regarding his published articles. When Hari noticed the bundle under his mattress, he decided to keep the money. He stole the money that was kept under the mattress during midnight when Anil was fast asleep. As soon as he left the hotel, he went to the railway station to catch a train to Lucknow. He missed the train and wandered around the city in search of it. He got soaked to the skin completely as it was pouring heavily.

As Hari was again feeling agitated and regretful, he began to regret stealing money from an honest man, such as Anil, who treated him well. The cheating Anil was his fault since he was taught how to read, write, and add numbers by him. Anil was devastated when Hari Singh suddenly changed his mind and decided to return to him. Despite the rainy weather, he kept the cash from where it was retrieved in the same spot. He woke up the following morning to find Anil was as normal as usual. Having earned fifty rupees, Hari was offered fifty rupees by the young man. A full month's payment as stated by Anil along with that statement. In any case, Hari realized the money was still moist when he touched it. Anil understood Hari's mistake the previous night but didn't treat him with disgust or turn him into the police despite being aware of it. Anil replaced this promise with a promise to teach Hari how to write full sentences. Hari Singh became a noble human being out of gratitude and respect for Anil after this incident.

Glossary:

1. Modest: Humble, not showing off or overly proud
2. Earnest: Serious and sincere
3. Fluttered: To move or flap quickly and lightly
4. Manipulative: Influencing someone unfairly or deceitfully
5. Reluctant: Hesitant or unwilling
6. Empathy: The ability to understand and share someone else's feelings
7. Conscience: An inner sense of right and wrong
8. Generosity: The quality of being kind and giving
9. Deceptive: Misleading or dishonest
10. Optimism: Hopefulness about the future

Choose the correct Answer:

1. Who is the narrator of the story?

a) Anil b) Hari Singh c) Ruskin Bond d) A police officer

2. What is Hari Singh's profession at the beginning of the story?

a) A writer b) A teacher c) A thief d) A shopkeeper

3. Why does Hari Singh decide to work for Anil?

a) He wants to learn how to write.

b) He is drawn to Anil's simplicity and honesty.

c) He sees Anil as an easy target for theft.

d) He is forced to by the police.

4. What is Anil's occupation?

a) A shopkeeper b) A journalist c) A writer d) A teacher

5. How does Anil react when Hari Singh offers to cook for him?

a) He immediately agrees.

b) He is hesitant but agrees after some thought.

c) He refuses outright.

d) He asks Hari for proof of his cooking skills.

6. How much money does Hari steal from Anil?

a) 500 rupees b) 1000 rupees c) 600 rupees d) 700 rupees

7. What causes Hari Singh to return the stolen money?

a) Fear of being caught by the police.

b) Anil's kindness and trust in him.

c) A desire for more money in the future.

d) Guilt over stealing from someone poor.

8. Where does Hari go after stealing the money?

a) To the railway station to board a train.

b) To a nearby village to hide.

c) To Anil's friend's house.

d) To the market to spend the money.

9. How does Anil react when he discovers Hari has returned the money?

a) He confronts Hari angrily.

b) He pretends not to know about the theft.

c) He reports Hari to the police.

d) He kicks Hari out of his house.

10. What lesson does the story convey?

a) Kindness and trust can change a person for the better.

b) Crime always pays in the end.
c) Dishonesty is the best policy.
d) Education has no value in life.

CHAPTER IV

UNIT IV
AS YOU LIKE IT
-SHAKESPEARE

About the author and text

As You Like It is a pastoral comedy by William Shakespeare believed to have been written in 1599 and first published in the First Folio in 1623. Shakespeare's company was originally called The Lord Chamberlain's Men and then, under King James, The King's Men. In a very real sense, this meant that his job was to please his wealthy and powerful patrons at court. "As You Like It" has some symbolic meanings, too, depending on your interpretation of the play. Love is the central theme of As You Like It, like other romantic comedies of Shakespeare. Following the tradition of a romantic comedy, As You Like It is a tale of love manifested in its varied forms. In many of the love-stories, it is love at first sight. Rosalind and her cousin escape into the forest and find Orlando, Rosalind's love. Disguised as a boy shepherd, Rosalind has Orlando woo her under the guise of "curing" him of his love for Rosalind. Rosalind reveals she is a girl and marries Orlando during a group wedding at the end of the play.

William Shakespeare's As You Like It, is a comedy thought to have been written in 1599. It follows the story of Rosalind, a heroine fleeing persecution. The play contains some of Shakespeare's most famous and well-known lines, many spoken by a character she meets in the Forest of Arden, Jacque As You Like It is one of the best romantic comedies of Shakespeare. In a romantic comedy, romantic and comic elements are mingled. The romantic elements delight and thrill, the comic elements make us laugh and forget our anxieties. Emotions, imaginations and fancy are common phenomenon of romantic comedy. As You Like It keeps us laughing most of the time, despite some saddling incidents in it. The laughter is aroused in us by Rosalind, Celia, by Touchstone, by Jaques.

There are some criteria of romantic comedy. They are first sight love, influence of nature, supernatural elements, role of forest, the romantic setting, happy ending and so on. In As You Like It, we see the first sight love between Rosalind and Orlando. The central theme of this play is love and marriage. This is the youthful love of Rosalind and Orlando. In romantic play nature plays a vital role. Nature dominates the human life. In As You Like It, we see the forest of Arden. Gradually all the characters come to the forest. Romantic comedy starts with love. There is a obstacle in the middle and a happy ending. According to Shakespeare, the course of true lover never did run smooth.

Summary

Sir Rowland de Bois has recently died, and, according to the custom of primogeniture, the vast majority of his estate has passed into the possession of his eldest son, Oliver. Although Sir Rowland has instructed Oliver to take good care of his brother, Orlando, Oliver refuses to do so. Out of pure spite, he denies Orlando the education, training, and property befitting a gentleman. Charles, a wrestler from the court of Duke Frederick, arrives to warn Oliver of a rumour that Orlando will challenge Charles to a fight on the following day. Fearing censure if he should beat a nobleman, Charles begs Oliver to intervene, but Oliver convinces the wrestler that Orlando is a dishonourable sportsman who will take whatever dastardly means necessary to win. Charles vows to pummel Orlando, which delights Oliver.

Duke Senior has been usurped of his throne by his brother, Duke Frederick, and has fled to the Forest of Ardenne, where he lives like Robin Hood with a band of loyal followers. Duke Frederick allows Senior's daughter, Rosalind, to remain at court because of her inseparable friendship with his own daughter, Celia. The day arrives when Orlando is scheduled to fight Charles, and the women witness Orlando's defeat of the court wrestler. Orlando and Rosalind instantly fall in love with one another, though Rosalind keeps this fact a secret from everyone but Celia. Orlando returns home from the wrestling match, only to have his faithful servant Adam warn him about Oliver's plot against Orlando's life. Orlando decides to leave for the safety of Ardenne. Without warning, Duke Frederick has a change of heart regarding Rosalind and banishes her from court. She, too, decides to flee to the Forest of Ardenne and leaves with Celia, who cannot bear to be without Rosalind, and Touchstone, the court jester. To ensure the safety of their journey, Rosalind assumes the dress of a young man and takes the name Ganymede, while Celia dresses as a common shepherdess and calls herself Aliena.

Duke Frederick is furious at his daughter's disappearance. When he learns that the flight of his daughter and niece coincides with the disappearance of Orlando, the duke orders Oliver to lead the manhunt, threatening to confiscate Oliver's lands and property should he fail. Frederick also decides it is time to destroy his brother once and for all and begins to raise an army.

Duke Senior lives in the Forest of Ardenne with a band of lords who have gone into voluntary exile. He praises the simple life among the trees, happy to be absent from the machinations of court life. Orlando, exhausted by travel and desperate to find food for his starving companion, Adam, barges in on the duke's camp and rudely demands that they not eat until he is given food. Duke Senior calms Orlando and, when he learns that the young man is the son of his dear former friend, accepts him into his company. Meanwhile, Rosalind and Celia, disguised as Ganymede and Aliena, arrive in the forest and meet a lovesick young shepherd named Silvius who pines away for the disdainful Phoebe. The two women purchase a modest cottage, and soon enough Rosalind runs into the equally lovesick Orlando. Taking her to be a young man, Orlando confides in Rosalind that his affections are overpowering him. Rosalind, as Ganymede, claims to be an expert in exorcising such emotions and promises to cure Orlando of lovesickness if he agrees to pretend that Ganymede is Rosalind and promises to come woo her every day. Orlando agrees, and the love lessons begin.

Meanwhile, Phoebe becomes increasingly cruel in her rejection of Silvius. When Rosalind intervenes, disguised as Ganymede, Phoebe falls hopelessly in love with Ganymede. One day, Orlando fails to show up for his tutorial with Ganymede. Rosalind, reacting to her infatuation with Orlando, is distraught until Oliver appears. Oliver describes how Orlando stumbled upon him in the forest and saved him from being devoured by a hungry lioness. Oliver and Celia, still disguised as the shepherdess Aliena, fall instantly in love and agree to marry. As time passes, Phoebe becomes increasingly insistent in her pursuit of Ganymede, and Orlando grows tired of pretending that a boy is his dear Rosalind. Rosalind decides to end the charade. She promises that Ganymede will wed Phoebe, if Ganymede will ever marry a woman, and she makes everyone pledge to meet the next day at the wedding. They all agree.

The day of the wedding arrives, and Rosalind gathers the various couples: Phoebe and Silvius; Celia and Oliver; Touchstone and Audrey, a goatherd he intends to marry; and Orlando. The group congregates before Duke Senior and his men. Rosalind, still disguised as Ganymede, reminds the lovers of their various vows, then secures a promise from Phoebe that if for some reason she refuses to marry Ganymede she will marry Silvius, and a promise from the duke that he would allow his daughter to marry Orlando if she were available. Rosalind leaves with the disguised Celia, and the two soon return as themselves, accompanied by Hymen, the god of marriage. Hymen officiates at the ceremony and marries Rosalind and Orlando, Celia and Oliver, Phoebe and Silvius, and Audrey and Touchstone. The festive wedding celebration is interrupted by even more festive news: while marching with his army to attack Duke Senior, Duke Frederick came upon a holy man who convinced him to put aside his worldly concerns and assume a monastic life. -Frederick changes his ways and returns the throne to Duke Senior. The guests continue dancing, happy in the knowledge that they will soon return to the royal court.

CHARACTER OF ROSALIND

Rosalind dominates As You Like It. So fully realized is she in the complexity of her emotions, the subtlety of her thought, and the fullness of her character that no one else in the play matches up to her. Orlando is handsome, strong, and an affectionate, if unskilled, poet, yet still we feel that Rosalind settles for someone slightly less magnificent when she chooses him as her mate. Similarly, the observations of Touchstone and Jaques, who might shine more brightly in another play, seem rather dull whenever Rosalind takes the stage.

The endless appeal of watching Rosalind has much to do with her success as a knowledgeable and charming critic of herself and others. But unlike Jaques, who refuses to participate wholly in life but has much to say about the foolishness of those who surround him, Rosalind gives herself over fully to circumstance. She chastises Silvius for his irrational devotion to Phoebe, and she challenges Orlando's thoughtless equation of Rosalind with a Platonic ideal, but still she comes undone by her lover's inconsequential tardiness and faints at the sight of his blood. That Rosalind can play both sides of any field makes her identifiable to nearly everyone, and so, irresistible.

Rosalind is a particular favourite among feminist critics, who admire her ability to subvert the limitations that society imposes on her as a woman. With boldness and imagination, she disguises herself as a young man for the majority of the play in order to woo the man she loves and instruct him in how to be a more accomplished, attentive lover—a tutorship that would not be welcome from a woman. There is endless comic appeal in Rosalind's lampooning of the conventions of both male and female behaviour, but an Elizabethan audience might have felt a certain amount of anxiety regarding her behaviour. After all, the structure of a male-dominated society depends upon both men and women acting in their assigned roles. Thus, in the end, Rosalind dispenses with the charade of her own character. Her emergence as an actor in the Epilogue assures that theatre goers, like the Ardenne foresters, are about to exit a somewhat enchanted realm and return to the familiar world they left behind. But because they leave having learned the same lessons from Rosalind, they do so with the same potential to make that world a less punishing place.

CHARACTER OF ORLANDO

According to his brother, Oliver, Orlando is of noble character, unschooled yet somehow learned, full of noble purposes, and loved by people of all ranks as if he had enchanted them (I.i.141–144). Although this description comes from the one character who hates Orlando and wishes him harm, it is an apt and generous picture of the hero of As You Like It. Orlando has a brave and generous spirit, though he does not possess Rosalind's wit and insight. As his love tutorial shows, he relies on commonplace clichés in matters of love, declaring that without the fair Rosalind, he would die. He does have a decent wit, however, as he demonstrates when he argues with Jaques, suggesting that Jaques should seek out a fool who wanders about the forest: "He is drowned in the brook. Look but in, and you shall see him," meaning that Jaques will see a fool in his own reflection (III.ii.262–263). But next to Rosalind, Orlando's imagination burns a bit less bright. This upstaging is no fault of Orlando's, given the fullness of Rosalind's character; Shakespeare clearly intends his audience to delight in the match. Time and again, Orlando performs tasks that reveal his nobility and demonstrate why he is so well-loved: he travels with the ancient Adam and makes a fool out of himself to secure the old man food; he risks his life to save the brother who has plotted against him; he cannot help but violate the many trees of Ardenne with testaments of his love for Rosalind. In the beginning of the play, he laments that his brother has denied him the schooling deserved by a gentleman, but by the end, he has proven himself a gentleman without the formality of that education.

CHARACTER OF DUKE SENIOR

The father of Rosalind and the rightful ruler of the dukedom in which the play is set. Having been banished by his usurping brother, Frederick, Duke Senior now lives in exile in the Forest of Ardenne with a number of loyal men, including Lord Amiens and Jaques. We have the sense that Senior did not put up much of a fight to keep his dukedom, for he seems to make the most of whatever life gives him. Content in the forest, where he claims to learn as much from stones and brooks as he would in a church or library, Duke Senior proves himself to be a kind and fair-minded ruler.

CHARACTER OF JAQUES

A faithful lord who accompanies Duke Senior into exile in the Forest of Ardenne. Jaques is an example of a stock figure in Elizabethan comedy, the man possessed of a hopelessly melancholy disposition. Much like a referee in a football game, he stands on the sidelines, watching and judging the actions of the other characters without ever fully participating. Given his inability to participate in life, it is fitting that Jaques alone refuses to follow Duke Senior and the other courtiers back to court, and instead resolves to assume a solitary and contemplative life in a monastery.

CHARACTER OF CELIA

The daughter of Duke Frederick and Rosalind's dearest friend. Celia's devotion to Rosalind is unmatched, as evidenced by her decision to follow her cousin into exile. To make the trip, Celia assumes the disguise of a simple shepherdess and calls herself Aliena. As elucidated by her extreme love of Rosalind and her immediate devotion to Oliver, whom she marries at the end of the play, Celia possesses a loving heart, but is prone to deep, almost excessive emotions.

CHARACTER OF DUKE FREDERICK

The brother of Duke Senior and usurper of his throne. Duke Frederick's cruel nature and volatile temper are displayed when he banishes his niece, Rosalind, from court without reason. That Celia, his own daughter, cannot mitigate his unfounded anger demonstrates the intensity of the duke's hatefulness. Frederick mounts an army against his exiled brother but aborts his vengeful mission after he meets an old religious man on the road to the Forest of Ardenne. He immediately changes his ways, dedicating himself to a monastic life and returning the crown to his brother, thus testifying to the ease and elegance with which humans can sometimes change for the better.

CHARACTER OF TOUCHSTONE

A clown in Duke Frederick's court who accompanies Rosalind and Celia in their flight to Ardenne. Although Touchstone's job, as fool, is to criticize the behavior and point out the folly of those around him, Touchstone fails to do so with even a fraction of Rosalind's grace. Next to his mistress, the clown seems hopelessly vulgar and narrow-minded. Almost every line he speaks echoes with bawdy innuendo.

CHARACTER OF OLIVER

The oldest son of Sir Rowland de Bois and sole inheritor of the de Bois estate. Oliver is a loveless young man who begrudges his brother, Orlando, a gentleman's education. He admits to hating Orlando without cause or reason and goes to great lengths to ensure his brother's downfall. When Duke Frederick employs Oliver to find his missing brother, Oliver finds himself living in despair in the Forest of Ardenne, where Orlando saves his life. This display of undeserved generosity prompts Oliver to change himself into a better, more loving person. His transformation is evidenced by his love for the disguised Celia, whom he takes to be a simple shepherdess.

CHARACTER OF SILVIUS

A young, suffering shepherd, who is desperately in love with the disdainful Phoebe. Conforming to the model of Petrarchan love, Silvius prostrates himself before a woman who refuses to return his affections. In the end, however, he wins the object of his desire.

CHARACTER OF PHOEBE

A young shepherdess, who disdains the affections of Silvius. She falls in love with Ganymede, who is really Rosalind in disguise, but Rosalind tricks Phoebe into marrying Silvius.

CHARACTER OF LORD AMIENS

A faithful lord who accompanies Duke Senior into exile in the Forest of Ardenne. Lord Amiens is rather jolly and loves to sing.

CHARACTER OF CHARLES

A professional wrestler in Duke Frederick's court. Charles demonstrates both his caring nature and his political savvy when he asks Oliver to intercede in his upcoming fight with Orlando: he does not want to injure the young man and thereby lose favor among the nobles who support him. Charles's concern for Orlando proves unwarranted when Orlando beats him senseless.

CHARACTER OF ADAM

The elderly former servant of Sir Rowland de Bois. Having witnessed Orlando's hardships, Adam offers not only to accompany his young master into exile but to fund their journey with the whole of his modest life's savings. He is a model of loyalty and devoted service.

CHARACTER OF SIR ROWLAND DE BOIS

The father of Oliver and Orlando, friend of Duke Senior, and enemy of Duke Frederick. Upon Sir Rowland's death, the vast majority of his estate was handed over to Oliver according to the custom of primogeniture.

CHARACTER OF CORIN

A shepherd. Corin attempts to counsel his friend Silvius in the ways of love, but Silvius refuses to listen.

CHARACTER OF AUDREY: A simpleminded goatherd who agrees to marry Touchstone.

CHARACTER OF WILLIAM: A young country boy who is in love with Audrey.

Glossary

1. **Exile**: The state of being banished from one's home or country
2. **Disguise**: The act of altering one's appearance to hide one's identity
3. **Jester**: A fool or clown who often uses humor to comment on social and political matters
4. **Courtly Love**: A medieval tradition of chivalrous love in which a knight or nobleman expresses adoration for a lady, often unattainable. Orlando's love for Rosalind follows this tradition.
5. **Soliloquy**: A speech given by a character alone on stage, revealing their innermost thoughts.
6. **Folly**: Foolishness or lack of sense
7. **Pastoral**: A literary work that idealizes rural life and nature
8. Court: The royal palace or the environment of the king and his advisors; the play contrasts the corrupt court with the more natural, free-spirited life in the forest.
9. **Romantic Comedy**: A genre of comedy that centers on the theme of love and often ends in marriage or reconciliation.

10. **Banished**: Expelled or forced to leave a place, especially a country or royal court. d and Duke Senior are both banished, leading them to find freedom and new identities in the forest.
11. **Wit**: The ability to use words and ideas in an intelligent and humorous way.
12. **Maidenhood**: The state of being a young woman or a virgin; often discussed in the context of Rosalind's love life and her ability to change identities.
13. **Allegory**: A story in which characters and events symbolize abstract ideas or themes.
14. **Shepherd**: A person who tends sheep
15. **Hymen**: The Greek god of marriage

Choose the correct Answer

1. Who is the Duke who is exiled in *As You Like It*?

a) Orlando b) Oliver c) Touchstone d) Duke Senior

2. Who does Rosalind fall in love with?

a) Orlando b) Oliver c) Touchstone d) Silvius

3. What disguise does Rosalind adopt when she flees to the Forest of Arden?

a) A shepherd b) A page boy c) A noblewoman d) A poet

4. Who is the jester in the play?

a) Amiens b) Touchstone c) Jaques d) Orlando

5. Which character says the famous line, "All the world's a stage"?

a) Orlando b) Jaques c) Duke Senior d) Rosalind

6. What is the name of Rosalind's cousin who accompanies her to the forest?

a) Phoebe b) Celia c) Audrey d) Silvia

7. Who does Oliver fall in love with?

a) Celia b) Phoebe c) Rosalind d) Audrey

8. What is the relationship between Duke Frederick and Duke Senior?
a) Brothers b) Father and son c) Friends d) Rivals

9. How does Touchstone, the jester, propose to marry Audrey

a) By convincing her with poetry b) By asking her father for permission
c) By offering her wealth d) By using wit and humor

10. How is the conflict between Duke Frederick and Duke Senior resolved?

a) Duke Frederick is defeated in battle by Orlando.
b) Duke Senior leaves the forest and returns to the court.
c) Duke Frederick relents and allows Duke Senior to return.
d) Duke Senior dies in the forest.

CHAPTER V

UNIT V
CONDITIONAL CLAUSES

Conditional sentences have two parts or clauses that give a condition in the dependent clause and a result in the independent clause. The condition clause usually contains an if statement. There are several different forms of conditional sentences that allow the writer to express various meanings using different tenses.

• Condition (if) clause + result clause

ZERO CONDITIONAL

The zero conditional uses the present tense in both clauses and is used to talk about something that is always or generally true. The present tense signifies that these actions are both possible and typical.

Form: If + simple present, simple present

Example 1: If it rains, I take an umbrella with me to work.

Example 2: If I wake up early, I always read in bed.

FIRST CONDITIONAL

The first conditional uses the present tense in the if clause and the future tense in the result clause. This form is used to talk about something that is a probable future result of a condition.

Form: If + simple present, will + base verb

Example 1: If I see you later, I will say hello.

Example 2: If I don't see you later, I won't be able to say hello.

SECOND CONDITIONAL

The second conditional uses the past tense in the if clause and a modal and base verb in the result clause. This form is used to talk about a hypothetical situation that cannot happen or is unlikely to happen.

Form: If + simple past, modal + base verb

Example 1: If I had a million dollars, I would buy a large vacation home.

Example 2: If I were you, I wouldn't wait to study for the test.

Note: The condition and the result are not taking place in the past, but the past tense is used to indicate the unreal nature of the situation.

THIRD CONDITIONAL

The third conditional uses the past perfect in the if clause and a modal and present perfect in the result clause. This form is used to talk about a hypothetical situation in the past that did not happen – typically with an outcome that did not happen and is perhaps the opposite of what did happen.

Form: If + past perfect, modal + present perfect

Example 1: If it had rained last week, the plants would not have died.

Example 2: If I had finished college, I would have become a doctor.

Choose the correct answer:

1. Which sentence correctly uses the first conditional?

A. If it rains, we would stay inside.

B. If it rains, we will stay inside.

C. If it rained, we will stay inside.

D. If it had rained, we would stay inside.

2. Identify the type of conditional clause in this sentence:

"If I were you, I would take the job."
A. Zero Conditional B. First Conditional C. Second Conditional D. Third Conditional

3. Choose the correct option to complete this third conditional sentence:

"If they ___ (prepare) better, they would have won the match."

A. prepare B. prepared C. had prepared D. were preparing

4. Which conditional form is used to express general truths or facts?

A. Zero Conditional B. First Conditional C. Second Conditional D. Third Conditional

5. Complete the sentence using the correct second conditional structure:

"If I ___ (win) the lottery, I would buy a mansion."
A. win B. won C. had won D. will win

RELATIVE CLAUSES

Relative Clauses: Restrictive and Non-Restrictive

Relative clauses are dependent clauses that modify a noun or pronoun. They are introduced by a relative pronoun such as *who, whom, which, that, whose,* etc. Relative clauses provide more information about a noun (called the antecedent) in the main clause. These clauses can be either **restrictive** or **non-restrictive.**

1. Restrictive Relative Clauses

A **restrictive relative clause** (also called a **defining relative clause**) provides essential information to identify the noun it modifies. This type of clause is necessary to the meaning of the sentence because it limits or restricts the meaning of the noun it describes. Without this clause, the sentence would lose important information or would be unclear.

- **Key Characteristics:**
  - **No commas**: Restrictive clauses are not set off by commas.
  - **Essential to meaning**: The information provided by the restrictive clause is needed to understand which person or thing is being referred to.
  - **Relative pronouns**: It can begin with *who*, *which*, *that*, *whose*.

Examples:

1. **The book that you gave me is amazing.**
   - The clause "that you gave me" restricts which book is being talked about (it's the book that was given, not any other book).
2. **The teacher who helped me passed away last year.**
   - The clause "who helped me" specifies which teacher is being referred to (the one who helped).
3. **The car which is parked outside is mine.**
   - "Which is parked outside" defines which car is being discussed, so the clause is necessary for understanding the subject.

4. **The artist whose paintings you admire is coming to town.**

    - The clause "whose paintings you admire" restricts which artist is being talked about (the one whose paintings are admired).

2. Non-Restrictive Relative Clauses

A **non-restrictive relative clause** (also called a **non-defining relative clause**) provides additional, non-essential information about a noun. The sentence would still make sense without this clause, as it only adds extra details. Non-restrictive clauses are typically used to give more information that is not critical to identifying the noun.

- **Key Characteristics:**

    - **Commas**: Non-restrictive clauses are always set off by commas.
    - **Non-essential information**: The information in a non-restrictive clause can be omitted without changing the fundamental meaning of the sentence.
    - **Relative pronouns**: It can begin with *who*, *which*, *whose*, or *where*.

Examples:

1. **My brother, who lives in New York, is coming to visit.**

    - The clause "who lives in New York" adds extra information about "my brother," but even without it, the main idea "My brother is coming to visit" remains clear.

2. **The Eiffel Tower, which is in Paris, is a famous landmark.**
    - "Which is in Paris" gives extra information about the Eiffel Tower, but it's not necessary to identify the landmark.
3. **The movie, which I watched last night, was fantastic.**
    - "Which I watched last night" adds more details about the movie, but it's not required to understand which movie is being referred to.
4. **Mrs. Smith, whose dog won a prize, is my neighbor.**
    - "Whose dog won a prize" provides extra information about Mrs. Smith, but the sentence still makes sense without it.

Feature	Restrictive Clause	Non-Restrictive Clause
Role in Sentence	Provides essential information, limits meaning	Provides additional, non-essential information
Commas	No commas used	Commas are used to set off the clause
Example	The book *that you gave me* is amazing.	My book, *which you gave me*, is amazing.
Meaning Without Clause	The meaning changes if the clause is removed	The main meaning remains the same if the clause is removed
Example with *that*	The house *that he bought* is big.	*The house, that he bought*, is big.

Differences Between Restrictive and Non-Restrictive Clauses

Use of That vs. Which in Restrictive and Non-Restrictive Clauses

- **In restrictive clauses,** *that* is typically used (though *which* can sometimes be used in less formal contexts).
  - Example: **The book that you recommended was great.**
- **In non-restrictive clauses,** *which* is always used, not *that*.
  - Example: **The book, which you recommended, was great.**

Choose the best answer:

1. What is a relative clause?

A. A clause that gives additional information about the subject or object.
B. A clause that connects two independent sentences.
C. A clause that always begins with "because."
D. A clause that expresses a condition.

2. Which sentence contains a relative clause?

A. She went to the park yesterday.
B. The book that you lent me was amazing.
C. I love cooking and reading.
D. He will come to the party tonight.

3. What word is commonly used to start a relative clause?

A. And B. But C. Who D. So

4. Identify the type of relative clause in this sentence:

"The car that I bought last week is very fast."
A. Restrictive relative clause B. Non-restrictive relative clause
C. Adverbial clause D. Main clause

5. Which of the following is a non-restrictive relative clause?

A. The man who is wearing a red shirt is my uncle.
B. My uncle, who is wearing a red shirt, is very kind.
C. The book that has a blue cover is my favorite.
D. The student who got the highest marks will receive an award.

6. Choose the correct relative pronoun to complete the sentence:

"She is the woman ___ I met at the conference."
A. which B. whose C. who D. whom

7. Fill in the blank to form a relative clause:

"The dog ___ tail is wagging looks happy."
A. who B. whose C. that D. which

8. Which sentence demonstrates correct use of a relative pronoun?

A. This is the book who I borrowed from Sarah.
B. The house, which was built in 1900, needs renovation.
C. I met a man, that is an artist, at the gallery.
D. The girl whom dress is blue is my sister.

PRECIS WRITING

Writing a precis means making an intelligent summary of a long passage. To write a precis one should have a clear understanding of the passage: only then well one be able to include all the essential points and tips and tricks of essay examples in the precis.

Some general considerations :

· A precis should be in the language of the precis-writer. The original passage is not to be reduced in length by just removing unimportant or unnecessary sentences and by reproducing the rest as the precis. It should be a brief gist or summary of the passage expressed in the writer's own words. A precis should be full i.e. it should contain all the essential thoughts, ideas or fact in the original passage. It should not contain repetitions or observations that are not relevant to the main theme of the original. A precis is always written in Reported Speech. The passage given may be a speech made by a person inDirect Speech, but the precis is to be in Reported Speech and in the Third Person and in the Past tense.

Techniques of Precis – Writing

There are three kinds of work to be done in producing a clear and successful precis. They are (1) Reading, (2) Writing and (3) Revision.

Reading

Read the passage carefully

If one reading is not enough to give you a general idea of its meaning, then read it a second time. As you read, find out the subject or the theme of the passage and what is said about the subject.

It will be a good thing if you find out the lead or the topic sentence. The lead sentence will help you to see the subject clearly. It will also help you to think of a title for the precis example.

Further reading may be necessary at this stage to make sure that the details of the passage are also understood. Read the passage more slowly this time, even sentence by sentence, and make sure that everything in the passage is understood. If this is not done, it is likely that you will miss something important, especially if it is expressed by a short phrase or a single word.

Now comes the process of selection. The writer of the precis writing passages has to decide what facts or ideas in the passage are essential and what are of secondary or no importance. Taking the main ideas of the passages as your point of reference, it should not be too difficult to write out the important points in the original in a corner of your writing work sheet.

Writing

You should first prepare a draft of the precis, keeping in mind, the need to reduce he original to one-third its length. The main thoughts expressed in the passage, the ideas it contains, the opinions presented and the conclusion arrived at should figure in the rough draft. Unimportant things like the names of people and places and dates should not figure in it.

It may so happen that your first draft is too long or that it sounds rather jerky. Shorten it if necessary and write out a careful second draft during college preparation. Sometimes you may need to work out three or even four drafts, but with reasonable care and concentration, you should normally succeed in producing a good precis writing by the second draft.

DENOTATION AND CONNOTATION

Denotation and connotation are two different aspects of the meaning of words, and understanding them helps to deepen our comprehension of language.

1. Denotation

Denotation refers to the **literal, primary, or explicit meaning** of a word—the definition that can be found in a dictionary. It is the objective meaning of the word, without any emotional or cultural associations. In essence, the denotation is the straightforward, factual meaning of a word.

- **Key Characteristics of Denotation:**
    - It is the **literal** meaning of a word.
    - It is **unambiguous** and commonly accepted.
    - It can be found in the **dictionary**.

Examples:

1. **Snake:**

  - **Denotation:** A long, legless reptile that slithers on the ground.

2. **Home:**
   - **Denotation:** A place where someone lives.

3. **Rose:**
   - **Denotation:** A type of flowering plant with thorny stems and typically red, pink, white, or yellow flowers.

2. Connotation

Connotation refers to the **additional meanings, feelings, emotions, or associations** that a word carries beyond its denotation. Connotations can be **positive**, **negative**, or **neutral**, and they are shaped by **cultural**, **social**, or **personal experiences**. Connotation involves the **subjective interpretation** of a word based on context.

- **Key Characteristics of Connotation:**
  - It includes **emotional** or **cultural associations** with a word.
  - It varies depending on **context**, **society**, and **individual perspectives.**
  - It can carry **positive**, **negative**, or **neutral** feelings.

Examples:

1. **Snake:**
   - **Connotation**: Often associated with **danger**, **deceit**, or **evil** (e.g., a "snake in the grass" implies a hidden threat or betrayal).
2. **Home:**
   - **Connotation**: May evoke feelings of **comfort**, **safety**, **belonging**, or **warmth**.
3. **Rose:**
   - **Connotation**: May symbolize **love**, **beauty**, or **romance**.

Difference Between Denotation and Connotation

Aspect	Denotation	Connotation
Definition	Literal, dictionary meaning	Additional meanings, feelings, or associations
Example	*Snake* = A legless reptile	*Snake* = Deception, danger, or evil
Context	Neutral and objective	Can vary based on context and culture
Impact	Does not evoke emotions or personal views	Evokes emotions, opinions, or judgments

Examples in Sentences

1. **Denotation of "Child":**

- "The **child** is playing outside."
    - **Denotation**: A young human being, typically below the age of adolescence.

Connotation of "Child":

- "The **child** is innocent and pure."
    - **Connotation**: The word "child" evokes feelings of **innocence** or **vulnerability**.

2. **Denotation of "Dog"**:

- "I have a **dog** at home."
    - **Denotation**: A domesticated carnivorous mammal, often kept as a pet.

Connotation of "Dog":

- "He's such a loyal **dog**."
    - **Connotation**: "Dog" here may carry the positive idea of **loyalty** or **companionship**.

How Denotation and Connotation Influence Language

- Writers, speakers, and advertisers often use **connotation** to create certain emotional responses in their audience. For example, using words with **positive connotations** like "freedom" or "equality" can inspire hope, while words with **negative connotations** like "war" or "poverty" can create sadness or concern.

- In literature, the **connotation** of words plays a crucial role in setting the tone and mood of a piece, while the **denotation** ensures clarity and precision in communication.

ONE-WORD SUBSTITUTIONS

One-word substitutions are used to replace a phrase with a single word that conveys the same meaning. They make sentences more concise and clear. Below is a list of common one-word substitutions along with their meanings:

1. A person who loves books: Bibliophile
2. A person who cannot speak: Mute
3. A person who cannot hear: Deaf
4. A person who writes books: Author
5. A person who does not believe in God: Atheist
6. A person who studies the stars and planets: Astronomer
7. A person who studies animals: Zoologist
8. A person who studies plants: Botanist
9. A person who studies human history: Historian
10. A person who studies the mind: Psychologist
11. A person who loves food: Gourmet
12. A person who loves himself/herself: Narcissist
13. A person who writes poems: Poet
14. A person who is always happy: Optimist
15. A person who is always sad: Pessimist

16. A person who betrays his country: Traitor
17. A person who is not afraid of danger: Daredevil
18. A person who repairs shoes: Cobbler
19. A person who makes furniture: Carpenter
20. A person who paints pictures: Artist
21. A person who makes statues: Sculptor
22. A person who deals with money: Banker
23. A person who sells books: Bookseller
24. A person who is an expert in law: Lawyer
25. A person who manages or owns a business: Entrepreneur
26. A person who studies or deals with laws: Jurist
27. A person who has great skill in a particular art or field: Virtuoso
28. A person who goes on foot: Pedestrian
29. A person who is overly concerned about cleanliness: Neurotic
30. A person who collects coins: Numismatis

Other Useful One-Word Substitutions

1. A story about imaginary beings: Fiction
2. A large destructive wave: Tsunami
3. A government by one person: Autocracy
4. A government by the people: Democracy
5. A group of musicians: Orchestra
6. A person who steals money from a bank: Bank robber
7. A person who collects stamps: Philatelist
8. A remedy for all diseases: Panacea
9. The study of the origin of words: Etymology
10. A place where fish are kept: Aquarium

11. A person who takes care of a library: Librarian
12. A government ruled by a king or queen: Monarchy
13. A group of lions: Pride
14. A thing that works automatically: Automaton
15. A disease that spreads rapidly: Epidemic
16. A medicine that kills bacteria: Antibiotic
17. A person who loves and studies nature: Naturalist
18. The first book of the Bible: Genesis
19. A place where sick animals are treated: Veterinary hospital
20. A system of government where religious leaders rule: Theocracy

CHAPTER VI

References

Bacon, Francis. "Of Adversity". *The Essays or Counsels, Civil and Moral.* Edited by John Pitcher, Penguin Classics, 1985.

Radhakrishnan, Sarvepalli. "Character Is Destiny." *The Present Crisis of Faith.* Hind Pocket Books, 1995.

Murthy, Sudha. "How I Taught My Grandmother to Read." *How I Taught My Grandmother to Read and Other Stories,* Penguin Books, 2004, pp. 1-5.

Dickinson, Emily. "There's Been Death in the Opposite House." *The Complete Poems of Emily Dickinson,* edited by Thomas H. Johnson, Little, Brown, 1960, p. 289.

Naidu, Sarojini. "The Soul's Prayer." *The Golden Threshold,* William Heinemann, 1905, pp. 23-24.

Blake, William. "London." *Songs of Experience,* 1794. Reprinted in *The Norton Anthology of English Literature,* edited by Stephen Greenblatt, vol. 2, 10th ed., Norton, 2018, pp. 111-12.7.

Poe, Edgar Allan. "The Purloined Letter." *Tales of Mystery and Imagination,* Wordsworth Editions, 1993, pp. 132-140.

Maugham, W. Somerset. "Mr. Know-All." *The Complete Short Stories of W. Somerset Maugham,* vol. 1, Penguin Books, 2000, pp. 18-32.

Bond, Ruskin. "The Thief's Story." *The Night Train at Deoli and Other Stories,* Penguin Books, 1988, pp. 45-50.

Shakespeare, William. *As You Like It.* Edited by Agnes Latham, Methuen Drama, 1975.

www.ingramcontent.com/pod-product-compliance
Lightning Source LLC
La Vergne TN
LVHW041116150826
845673LV00007B/2073

* 9 7 9 8 8 9 6 3 2 5 9 6 3 *